History of Swansea

AND OF THE

Lordship of Gower

VOLUME II

*From the fourteenth to
the seventeenth centuries*

BY

WILLIAM HENRY JONES

*Formerly Librarian and Director of
the Royal Institution of South Wales*

First Published 1992

ISBN 0 9508517 2 8

and

0 9508517 1 X (hard cover)

Published by the Royal Institution of South Wales,
Swansea.

Typeset in Elante 10 on 12.

Printed by Gwasg Morgannwg, Neath Abbey.

PREFACE

W. H. Jones, a leading figure amongst past historians of Swansea, died in 1932. Volume I of his *History of Swansea and the Lordship of Gower* had appeared in 1920, but Volume II was still only at the proof-reading stage at the time of his death. Although hopes were then expressed that it would soon be published these were not fulfilled, but the proofs were eventually acquired by the University College of Swansea and housed in the College Library. Several members of the Royal Institution of South Wales and other researchers have found the original documents extensively quoted by W. H. Jones in this work to be of considerable value for the study of local history.

The Royal Institution has, therefore, filled the gap in his works by the publication of Volume II of his *History*, even though his text is more than sixty years old. There is now more interest than ever in local history, and, in particular, the history of Swansea and of Gower. The Royal Institution of South Wales is pleased to publish this book as a sincere tribute to the man who was for many years its Librarian and the Director of its Museum.

The co-operation of the University College of Swansea, through their Librarian, Miss M. I. Cooper, in permitting publication of the proofs of this work is much appreciated. The support and endorsement of Mr. Anthony Hughes of Langland, the historian's great-nephew, is also most welcome.

Bernard Morris

President, The Royal Institution of South Wales.

1992.

CONTENTS

INTRODUCTION

In the first volume of his *History of Swansea and the Lordship of Gower,* published in 1920, W. H. Jones took the story from prehistoric times, through the Roman period and the Dark Ages, to the coming of the Normans. He then dealt in detail with the counter attacks on the area by the Welsh princes which often brought devastation to the town and its castle. He traced carefully the fortunes of the lords who ruled Gower virtually as a private kingdom, and their involved legal (and sometimes military) struggles with the crown and with each other. His final chapters brought his story down to the opening years of the 1300s, ending with the death of William de Breos (third of that name to have held Gower), a turbulent character whose complicated schemes for disposing of his lordship to several persons at once went badly wrong, and provided one of the causes which ultimately led to revolt and to the death of King Edward II. It is with the desperate flight of that king to Glamorgan, his temporary stay at Neath while he tried to raise the men of Gower to come to his help, and his capture not far away, that the second volume of W. H. Jones' history opens.

Amongst the general narrative his first volume included a number of direct translations of charters and other original documentary sources for the history of our area. Volume II makes even more use of such sources and it is these, even when superficially appearing to be dry law cases and mere financial accounts, which provide an intimately detailed picture of local life to which we can still relate even after so many centuries. When the unfortunate King Edward II failed to raise a military force from his last base at Neath, he sent his royal baggage, treasure and court records to Swansea Castle for safekeeping. The king's goods were of immense value, and were conveyed to Swansea by the governor of the castle and a strong force of local men. It is clear that these, and others, took full advantage of the troubled times and the fall of the king to share out the royal treasure and to disperse it far and wide. It is certain that such a valuable windfall has not been seen in Gower before or since. However, the old king's treasure was automatically the new king's treasure, and five years later, when Edward III was firmly in control, a formal enquiry was held to find the missing treasure, and in particular *who* had taken *what.* The lengthy record of the findings of the enquiry are set out in full in our author's pages, and tell us in detail of the wealth which accompanied a king of England on his travels around the kingdom, even when his cause was lost. It also tells us the names and status of many local people, Welsh and English, who had worked together closely in the cause of taking what they could. The enquiry was no doubt a great disappointment to them.

It is details of local life and happenings such as these, though rarely on such a grand scale, which can be found time and time again in these translated extracts in W. H. Jones' pages, linked and explained by his narrative and by his very full notes. Here are some of the earliest records of the names of Swansea's streets, including High Street, "Seintmarie Strete" and "Fischeris Strete" (the latter, Fisher Street, now included in Princess Way, together with Goat Street, another ancient name). Repairs to Swansea Castle in expectation of attack by the supporters of Owain Glyndwr are referred to in the very full financial accounts for the years 1400 to 1403. As well as describing the work carried out by masons and carpenters, and listing the payments to men at arms and archers guarding the castle, these accounts include such fine detail as the arrangements for providing firewood to warm the accountants in their rooms at the castle and even the purchase of the parchment on which these accounts were written.

Later on, from 1478, we can read other accounts referring to the repair of the local watermills (including the two at Brynmill), and to the rents of fishing weirs in the river and bay, together with a former smelting house "near the castle" which had been owned by Henry Conneway. With many more details of this sort, W. H. Jones takes this second volume of his *History* through three centuries in the life of Swansea and Gower, to close in the middle of the seventeenth century. Those wishing to follow his account down to the twentieth century will find no Volume Three as such, but the apparent gap had already been ably filled by his notable work entitled *The History of the Port of Swansea* which was published in 1922. In dealing with the rise of the port and Swansea's trade W. H. Jones covered many aspects of the growth of Swansea and its neighbourhood as an industrial centre, so, in many respects, completing his detailed account of local history from the earliest times to the present century. With the publication of Volume II the break in the story caused by his death has now been filled.

The walled town of Swansea in the period described in this volume (and, indeed, until barely two hundred years ago) occupied only the very centre of the modern city. In terms of present landmarks, it covered only the area from the Strand to a little beyond Princess Way, and from the bottom of Wind Street to the point where Morris Lane and King Street cross High Street, just past the Bush Hotel. The town may have been small, but Gower covered then (as, for parliamentary purposes it does today) an area extending far beyond the present peninsula. On the west, its boundary was the Burry estuary and the Llwchwr river. From near modern Ammanford the boundary then ran eastwards along the valleys of the Amman and the Twrch to reach the site of Ystalyfera, then followed the Tawe to the sea at Swansea. At some time around 1300 a border conflict resulted in the boundary near Ammanford being pushed south to the Cathan brook, where it remains to this day. On the east bank of the Tawe near Swansea was the area known as Kilvey, extending eastwards as far as the middle of Crymlyn Bog and on the north reaching Mynydd Drumau, and this area was always held with the lordship of Gower, although technically separate from it. When the sources quoted by W. H. Jones refer to "Gower" and to "the men of Gower," it is the large area of the whole lordship which is meant, not just the Gower peninsula.

In medieval times, the lordship of Gower was divided into two broad divisions, the Englishery and the Welshery, Gower Anglicana and Gower Wallicana repectively. In the first, English/Norman settlement was substantial and land-holding was governed by the law and custom of the invaders, while in the second the population remained almost wholly Welsh in origin and land was held by native custom, subject to the overall rule of the lord of Gower. As a very rough guide, the division between the two parts of the lordship ran through Cwmbwrla to Pontarddulais, with the Welsh area to the north and the English to the south. This simple picture is, however, complicated by the presence of some English manors north of this line (including the important manor of Trewyddfa, kept in the lord's own hands), and large areas of Welsh tenure south of it, particularly along the north side of the peninsula towards Penclawdd. This was the area known as Gower Wallicana Subboscus, i.e. Welsh Gower 'below the wood', the wood which ran in a broad band across the neck of the peninsula from the Tawe to Loughor.

Places in all of these areas are referred to in this volume, most being identifiable, but some still a mystery to us. Many of the spellings in the quotations from original documents will seem strange, and appear in several versions as there was of course no standardised spelling. Most, however, can soon be 'translated' to their more familiar modern forms, often now represented in the names of Swansea's suburbs. For modern place-names, W. H. Jones' versions have been kept even where more correct versions are now in formal use, e.g. his 'Llanelly' for our 'Llanelli'. This retains the flavour of his writing, and is in keeping with his style, which was that of the early part of the present century rather than that of the end. Having accepted that, the modern reader will soon find the story he tells and the documents he quotes so extensively are full of human interest, excitement and 'colour' (= violence at a safe distance ?) .

History itself is not a static thing, and since W. H. Jones wrote research has continued and much has been published. Some of our author's comments and conclusions would need some modification if they were part of a 'new' account of Swansea's history, but his work is now published as *he* wrote it, and in his own words. For more recent news and views on such matters, the reader is referred to the Appendix on page 90 where various relevant books and papers are listed.

With or without these later works his *History* stands on its own merits, bringing to life three hundred years of local events, incidents and personalities, more than enough to provide the plots for a dozen historical romances set in Swansea and the lordship of Gower.

B.M.

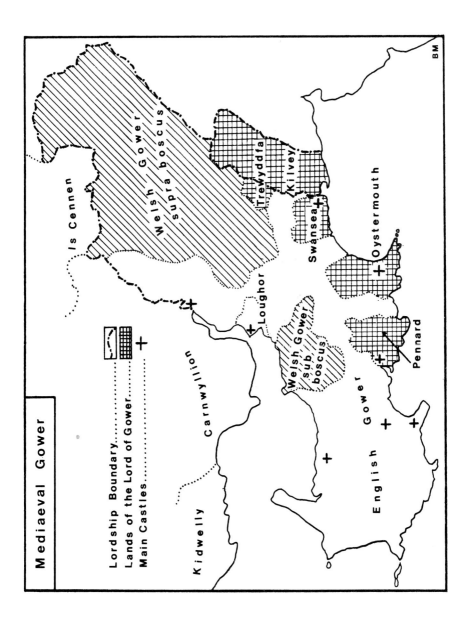

Mediaeval Gower

Lordship Boundary..........
Lands of the Lord of Gower......
Main Castles...............

Is Cennen

Welsh Gower supra boscus

Trewyddfa

Kilvey

Swansea

Oystermouth

Loughor

Carnwyllion

Welsh Gower sub boscus

Pennard

Kidwelly

English Gower

BM

xi

W. H. Jones.

(A photograph published in 1896.)

W. H. JONES
An Outline Biography

Returning to his native Swansea in 1913 after a successful career as a journalist and newspaper editor in various parts of Britain, William Henry Jones soon gained a reputation as one of the town's leading historians. In 1920 he qualified for a substantial entry in *Who's Who in Wales,* and he has an honourable mention in the *Dictionary of Welsh National Biography.* These sources supply the most accessible information about his life and work, but they can be supplemented by information from official records, contemporary articles, correspondence and from the dates and titles of his own publications.

He was born on the 4th February 1860, the third child (and second son) of another William Henry Jones, a confusingly common Swansea name, and his wife Anne (née Fisher). She had been born in Northumberland, but his father's birthplace was Swansea. When W. H. Jones junior was born his parents were living at 78 Oxford Street, where they had a wine and spirit shop, which by the 1870s had become a grocers shop. It stood on the north side of Oxford Street, between Portland Street and Union Street, facing the wall of Swansea Market, and was typical of the three-storey terraced houses built in large numbers in the centre of the town as it expanded in the early nineteenth century. Soon converted into shops, many of them, including our historian's birthplace, had been rebuilt by the end of the century and were then destroyed in the February 1941 air raids. Shops from the post-war redevelopment period now stand on the site.

His natural interest in history and an aptitude for writing and publishing books and pamphlets was soon evident. Four of these, including his *History of Swansea Castle,* had been published by 1879 while W. H. Jones was still in his teens and before his journalistic career took him away from Swansea for over thirty years. It was, however, not only Swansea's history that appealed to him and it seems that wherever his career took him he would soon be researching in depth into the records of the locality. From the list of his publications which appears at the end of Volume I of his *History of Swansea* in 1920 it is possible to chart where he worked at various periods of his career. Some of these were pamphlets but others were substantial volumes which required much research and an understanding of the local area. From these it appears that he was in North Wales in 1879-84 (writing on Criccieth, Carnarvon, Conway and Bangor); in Suffolk in 1887-92 (three volumes on Bury St. Edmunds — also *The Vale of Neath: a Holiday-sketch for East Anglians*); Exeter in 1893-95 (editor, *Exeter Flying Post*); Norwich in 1896-1901 (editor, *Norfolk*

Chronicle); and Great Yarmouth in 1903-07 (*Eastern Morning Gazette*). In 1912 he was being thanked for his work in connection with "The Festival of Empire" and in the following year he returned to Swansea, at the age of fifty-three.

Here he was soon appointed Librarian and Director at the Swansea Museum of the Royal Insitution of South Wales, and also became the Honorary Archivist to the Corporation of Swansea. The first volume of his *History of Swansea* appeared in 1920, soon followed, in 1922, by his unrivalled work on the growth of the harbour and port. His proposals for publishing the extensive early archives of the Corporation of Swansea could not be carried out, unfortunately, but throughout the 1920s his frequent local lectures and newspaper articles on Swansea's past reached an appreciative public and his name, and knowledge, became widely known. When he died in March 1932 the *South Wales Evening Post* commented that W. H. Jones had been engrossed in historical subjects from the days of his boyhood, when he had come under the influence of Lieut. Colonel George Grant Francis (historian, town councillor, mayor, driving-force in the founding of the Royal Institution and much else in Swansea in the nineteenth century), "in whose steps he was to follow so admirably."

W. H. Jones would have sought no greater tribute.

Oxford Street in 1862, looking eastwards from Union Street.

W. H. Jones' father's shop, No. 78, is the white-fronted building immediately to the right of the "Teague's" sign. Our future historian, then two years old, would have been living there at the date of this photograph.

The wall of the town's market, with the many chimneys of its butcher's stalls, is on the right of the picture.

Swansea Museum Collection

CHAPTER I

HOW KING EDWARD II.'S PROPERTY WAS LOOTED AT SWANSEA

EFORE pursuing further the history of the Lordship of Gower, we must retrace our steps in the chronology of events in order to record the circumstances which connected Edward II. with Swansea.

On the 10th September, 1312, the king granted a charter to William de Breos confirming him in his lordship of Gower at the request of Aylmer de Valence, earl of Pembroke. Ten days later, on the 20th September, 1312, the king also confirmed to Swansea the charter granted to it by Henry III., and as we find Aylmer de Valence amongst the witnesses to the deed, it is probable that it was to him that the town owed this fresh municipal advantage also.

The charter is wonderfully preserved both as to parchment and writing, and a considerable portion of the great seal still hangs to the document—a sharp impression of the handsome seal done in green wax. The parchment is 12¾ inches wide by 9 inches deep. The charter is an inspeximus, and naturally recites the earlier charter, and this having been already printed (Vol. i., p. 244) it has been deemed unnecessary to repeat it here. The other portions of the charter are as follows:—

Edward, by the grace of God, king of England, lord of Ireland, and duke of Aquitain, To the archbishops, bishops, abbots, priors, earls, barons, justices, sheriffs, reeves, ministers, and all his bailiffs and faithful people, greeting, WE HAVE INSPECTED the charter which the Lord Henry of famous memory, heretofore king of England, our grandfather, made to the burgesses of Sweyneshie, in these words: HENRY, by the grace of God king of England, lord of Ireland, duke of Normandy *(and so on, word for word, to the end of King Henry's charter as printed at Vol. i., p. 244)*: Now, we, the grant and confirmation aforesaid, ratifying and approving the same for us and our heirs, as much as in us is, do grant and confirm as the said charter of our said grandfather doth reasonably testify. These being witnesses: the venerable father W., bishop of Worcester; and J., bishop of Bath and Wells; Aylmer de Valence, earl of Pembroke; Hugh le Despenser, Nicholas de Segrave, Edmund de Mauley, steward of our household; William de Montacute and others. Given by our hand at Windsor, the twentieth day of September, in the sixth year of our reign. (1312).

Upon the death of the elder Despenser, the earl of Winchester, at Bristol, the lordship of Gower reverted to King Edward II.[1] This was in 1326, when the king was endeavouring to evade capture at the hands of his queen and the prince of Wales (soon to become Edward III.). The flight of the king, with his only surviving favourite the younger Despenser, brought him to Glamorgan, and on the 5th November from Margam to Neath.

Doubtless it was the king's close associations with the lordship that led him to include in a little embassy[2] of intercession on his behalf, which he despatched from Neath to the queen, Rhys ap Griffith, the steward of Gower; and whilst this little party was proceeding to Hereford on its mission, Edward issued at Neath, a writ[3] for raising all the horse and foot forces of Gower, as part of his effort to surround himself with an efficient body-guard.

This mandate was of a piece with the panic-sticken orders issued by the king since 1324. In that year, consequent on Isabella's escape with her paramour to France, the 'bailiffs' of Swansea had been notified to hold up all ships of the port, and all craft entering here, capable of carrying 40 tons and more, and equip them for the king's service.

In December, 1325, they were ordered to search all ships entering Swansea harbour, or wishing to leave for beyond seas, and to arrest any persons bearing letters prejudicial to the king; for only by such general search at sea-ports could communication with the queen in France be prevented.

In January, 1326, a similar order, extending to horses, arms, gold and silver, was received by the Swansea 'bailiffs,' who were to allow such goods to be sent from the port only by accredited merchants. And then, in August, they were further ordered to cause the owners of ships of the port, of 50 tons burthen and upwards, to bring them, provided with arms, victuals, and other necessaries, with double equipment, for the king's service to France; whilst owners of smaller vessels were not to leave Swansea for any purpose under pain of imprisonment.[4]

During the king's stay at Cardiff, on the 27th October, he had taken further steps to secure his safety. He has notified his ministers in Magor and Wentllwch, of a levy which was to be made on men in the parts of Glamorgan and Monmouth, and he assigned to Ieuan ap Meuryk and Ieuan ap Morgan the raising of men in the lands of Nedeslonde and Kilueye (Neath and Kilvey).[5] Two days later, from Caerphilly, the king notified his ministers in Pembrokeshire and the adjoining country that he had authorised Rhys ap Griffith to levy men there. Amongst those also named in the document were Robert de Penres and Robert de Pembrugge, who were directed to raise forces in the land of Gower and the adjacent parts, the former being also responsible for the levy in Haverford and its neighbourhood.[6]

On the 4th November, from Margam, a notice was issued to the king's ministers of Glamorgan and parts adjoining, that the king has assigned the custody of all the ports on the sea-coast between the rivers Taff and Tawe to persons who are named therein.

Arriving at Neath on the 5th November, the king appealed beseechingly to the men of Gower to come to his aid, but apparently in vain. Robert de Penres, Robert de Pembrugge, John de Langeton, and Richard Wolf were

2

empowered 'to raise all the forces of the lordship of Gower, horse and foot, who were to proceed to the king for the purpose of marching, at his wages, against the enemies and rebels.'

On the 6th November the men of Gower were notified that John de Langeton, Peter de la Bere, and William de Oth yn Goure' were authorised to see to the defence of the town of Sweneseye; and they were to be given every faciltiy to provide the town with victuals, ammunition, etc. Also a commission was issued to John de Langeton, appointing him seneschal, or steward, of Gower; and he and Richard Wolf were also ordered to seize for the king all lands and tenements of the late Hugh le Despenser, earl of Winchester, which he had held of the king in Gower.[7]

The king had hoped for a favourable consideration of the appeal of his embassy to the queen, but when they returned to report failure, panic seized him and his followers. The last date of the records of his little court at Neath is the 10th November, and upon that day, probably, all his chancery papers and other impedimenta were despatched to Swansea Castle, the king apparently intending to follow them there, in the hope of finding safety in the defences set up by De Langeton and others. But he remained yet a week at Neath, for the queen, having despatched Henry, earl of Lancaster, and others to take the king, he was captured at Neath on the 16th November. The *Vita Edwardi Secundi auctore Malmesberensi* states that he was taken 'apud Neythe in Westwallia,' and the *Vita et Mors Ed. II.*, of Thomas de la Moore (both these works are published in the *Edwardian Chronicles* of the Rolls Series), affirms that he was captured 'in monasterio de Niethe,' though other authorities place his arrest at or near the town of Llantrisant.[8]

And now as to the chancery rolls that had been removed to Swansea. A memorandum entered in the fines roll, 22 November, 20 Edward II. (1326), mentions the finding of a large number of documents in Swansea castle by Sir William la Zouche, who was also one of those who, 'by large gifts bestowed on the Welshmen (as Hollinshed tells us), were able to seize King Edward and the junior Despenser.[9] The rolls had been in the custody of Master Henry de Clif, the keeper of the rolls of the king's chancery; and it is stated that they were removed from Swansea by the two St. Johns, Sir John and Sir Edward, to the chamber of Queen Isabella in the bishop's palace at Hereford, where she was lodging.[10] Not all the documents were recovered, however, and an enormous quantity of plate also remained behind to be 'appropriated' by the families of Gower and the district.

On the 18th July, 1331, Edward III, issued a commission to Richard de Peshale (who had married Alina de Breos, widow of John de Mowbray, and of whom more later) and Edmund Trussel, whose place however was taken by David de la Bere,[11] to inquire as to the goods and jewels of the late king, which were alleged to have been stolen by some 'malefactors' at Swayneseye. Sir Robert de Penres, knight, of Oxwich (and of Penrice, son of another Sir Robert whose wife was a daughter of Morgan Gam), had been indicted for the offence, but had been released on mainprise; and the commissioners were directed to restore his goods and chattels to him.

The inquisition was taken at Swansea in four stages. At the first, held on Monday next after the feast of the exaltation of the Holy Cross, it was ascertained that a quantity of plate, arms, and other goods specified in the record[12] was sent from Neath to Swansea in the custody of John de Langton,[13] custodian, or governor, of Swansea Castle and the whole land of Gower.[14] Amongst the inhabitants of the Welshery of the lordship and the neighbourhood, who are mentioned as having assisted in the transportation of the same by John de Langton's consent, are Phi' Res, Res Dwy,[15] Willi le Hunte,[16] another John de Langton, Robert Maunxel,[17] Hamund Turbirvill; John David,[18] and William ap Walter Vaughan, Richard le Wolf[19] and Robert de la Manis (?Mare), William le Porter, Adam le Coron'r, Henry Durant, Richard de Penrees, Richard Scurlag, Richard Manxel, Howel ap Thomas, Evan ap Eynon and John his son, Eynon Vaghan, Howel Voab, Morgan ap Meuric, Thomas Blew, Walter le Box, and John Bernard, and Robert Dun.

This first inquiry, and also the second, were confined to the examination of witnesses from the Welshery of Gower, whose names appear in the record. In addition to those already named, there were examined the following witnesses:— John Testardus, sen., Richard de Wells, Robert de Penrigg, John Phillip, Philip Res, Peter de la Bere, John de Horton,[20] John Duphous, Richard de Boterwyk, Henrici de Ditton, Philip, rector of Penmaen,[21] Simon de Reding,[22] Richard Wadekyn (?Watkin), Will' Legat, Roger le Chaundeler, Cadogan ap Griffith, and William and Griffith his brothers, William ap Cadogan, Jevan ap Goulhaved and his five sons, Gilbert Talbot, and Griffith de Cauntyngton, archdeacon of Kermerdyn.

As an indication of what had happened, it may be related that Res Dwy was found to be in possession of harness (as armour was, thus early, called), silver vases, vestments, jewels, and other goods, silver and gold, valued at £400; William le Hunter had a robe, a sword, bow and twelve arrows, etc., value £120; John Langton had, in silver vessels, noble vestments, choice armour, linen, money, etc., £300; Robert Maunxel had 30s.; Richard le Wolf, £100; John and William ap Walter Vaughan, each £20; John Testard, sen., 2 habergeons (see glossary on page 6), 1 bacinet with an aventail, 1 capel de vinbrer, a pair of boots, a hood, knife, and saddle, value 103s. 3d.; John Phelipp, 5s.; John de Horton had a pair of gloves of plate, a silver pitcher, haketons, pair of gauntlets, etc. The total value of the spoils revealed at the end of the second inquisition was £2472 9s. 11d.

4

At the third stage of the inquiry, held before the same commissioners, on the following Saturday, many of the burgesses of Swaynes' were examined, and reference is made to the following persons, besides many of those already mentioned:— Roger de Bosenho (constabularius de Kedwelli et Karnwal'am dictum castrum de Sweynes'), John Smale and others of his family, Sir Walter le Box, Jevan ap Gellawce, David Petous, Walter Bougan, Patric ap Meuric, Howell ap Elydir, Philip Hervey, Richard Wrench, Robert Carman, John Quart, John de la Mare of Sweynes', Walter le Wyse, Henry Doraunt, Thomas Skynner, Thomas Eliot, John Leys, Robert Wrench, Thomas de la Veese, John Sepere,[23] and Griffith ap Ph' ap Gwillym.

The evidence taken at this third inquiry shewed that our burgesses had reaped a considerable harvest of the unfortunate king's goods. The people of the castle had evidently joined in the appropriation of the spoils. It was found that Roger de Bosenho, constable of Kidwelly, had entered the castle of Sweynes', had there despoiled the 'treasure' of John Smale and his family, and had taken two horses, armour, silver vessels, etc., to the value of £100. The same Roger and Sir Walter le Box had part of the goods belonging to the late king's chaplain, vestments, vessels of silver, etc., valued at £20; Richard le Wolf had 3 capellae de visura, with their appendages, one gesoeround and one hakeney; Richard Wrench had a horn worth 40s.; Robert Carman, a pair of knives worth 40d.; John Quart, a horn worth 9d. John Testard, a saddle, a habergeon, pair of gauntlets, and other goods, worth 40s. The men of Gower had taken harness and other goods from the castle of Sweynes' and from the custody of De Langton, to the value of £60; Philip de Sweneseie (the rector of Penmayn) had had two horses, one of which he (pious man that he was) sent back, but the other he had sold to John de Horton for 24s.; John de la Mare de Sweynes' had a horse value 105s.; Walter le Wyse two horses, a robe, haketon, basenet, and other goods, valued at 40s.; Howell ap Thomas, a horse, silver vessels, arms, etc., value 100s.; John Seys, a vessel of silver, arms, etc., value £10; John de Penress, a horse which Philip Knayt[24] took in the castle of Sweynes', value 4 marks, and the total of the goods traced at this third stage of the inquiry was £661 7s. 7d.

The fourth and concluding inquiry was taken at Sweyneseye before the same persons, on the Tuesday after Michaelmas, the same year. There is in the record much repetition of that concerning the first stage, including the statement that some of the plate, armour, and other goods were transported from Neath to Swansea by Roger de Bosenho, Walter le Box, Cadogan ap Griffith, Jevan ap Gollaved. and other men of Kidwelly and Carnwallaun, by the consent of John de Langton, in whose custody the goods had been placed. And thus the inquisition concludes.

5

Ten years later, 20th April, 10 Edw. III., 1336, a royal commission was appointed to enquire by jury in Glamorgan and Morgannok for information regarding the malefactors and disturbers of the peace who had in their hands treasure consisting of plate of gold and silver, jewels, arms, victuals, and other things to the value of some sixty thousand pounds, and endeavour to regain possession of the same. The object of this enquiry was doubtless to recover such of the late king's effect as had been scattered along the route of his flight through Glamorgan, but after the lapse of ten years, in a wild country like this, there must have been little hope of retrieving any of them.

There is just one somewhat obscure detail which we think it well to add. The inquisition has revealed the circumstance that the plate, arms, and other goods referred to therein had been sent from Neath to Swansea. We are led to wonder if there is any connection between this accumulation of treasure and that stated to have been lost by the king on his capture at Neath. The statement we refer to is a significant marginal note, added to the original MS. of the *Annales Paulini*,[25] as follows:— 'Dominus Rex captures perdidit in Castello de Neys (Neath) xiii. milia librarum.' It is a question whether the £13,000 was cash or value; and if the latter, did represent the plate then stored at Neath Castle and brought to Swansea, and which became the subject of the inquiry of 1326?

Brief glossary for pages 4 & 5

Aventail	Chain-mail protection for the neck and shoulders.
Bacinet	Tall open-fronted helmet.
Capel de visura	Protective metal skull-cap, with face guard.
Habergeon	Sleeveless coat of chain-mail.
Haketon	Quilted garment worn with armour.

[1] *Vide* Vol. i., p. 341-2 (where 1325 is printed in error for 1326).

[2] King Edward's embassy to Queen Isabella, comprised: the Abbot of Neath, Res ap Griffith, Edward de Bohun, Oliver de Burdegala, and John de Harsik. Their safe conduct was dated at Neath, the 10th November, 1326. (See *Arch. Camb.*, 5th Series, Vol. iv., p. 172.)

[3] *Rot. Pat.*, 20 Edward II., r. 7; probably one of the rolls recovered from Swansea Castle a little later.

[4] In 1328 an order came through to Swansea, enjoining all owners and masters of ships of less than 40 tons burthen, that were away from the port, to be brought back, lest the malefactors from Normandy and Poitou take them.

[5] Clark's *Cartae*, 1910 ed., p. 2361.

[6] *Ibid.*, p. 2364.

[7] *Vide* Rev. John Griffith's *Edward II. in Glamorgan* (1904), pp. 198-9.

[8] Dr. Stubbs, in his introduction to the *Chron. Edw. 1. and II.* (8vo., 1883, Rolls ed., p. xcvi.), endeavours to prove 'Llantrissaint' to have been the place where the king was captured. The *Ann. Paulini* spell the word 'Lantrosin' (Vol. i., p. 319), and Walsingham gives 'Laturssan' (Vol. i., p. 184).

[9] William la Zouch benefitted largely by the fall of young Despenser, for he immediately became custos of the lordship of Glamorgan, and married Despenser's widow, Alianor or Eleanor, the elder De Clare heiress. The patent roll of 4 Edward III. (mem. 4) informs us that this William, and Eleanor Despenser his wife, had been bound in the vast sum of £50,000, on the security of Eleanor's inheritance, to obtain pardon for the theft by Eleanor of a great quantity of jewels, florins, and other goods at the Tower of London.

[10] It is interesting to know, in connection with Queen Isabella, that five hundred years later, that is early in the eighteen-hundreds, there lived in Swansea a clever doctor, Dr. David Nicol, amongst whose patients were a couple in humble circumstances whom he restored to health, but who found themselves unable to pay any fee. In token of their gratitude to him, however, they asked his acceptance of a small oaken box containing some ancient parchments with seals appended, upon which they looked as somewhat of a curiosity. When the local Museum was formed by the Royal Institution of South Wales, the box and its contents were deposited there, and one of the documents proved to be the original contract of affiance between Prince Edward and Isabella, princess of France, dated 1303. There seems to be no doubt· that this document was one of those brought to Swansea amongst the personal papers of the king, and it now reposes in the Institution named.

[11] David de la Bere, of Gower, son of Sir John is mentioned in the inquisition of 1319, concerning De Breos' alienation of Gower properties. The following pedigree is taken from the Jenkins MS. pedigrees in the library of the Royal Institution of South Wales (p. 370b) : De la Bere of Weobly Castle. (1) Sir John De la Bere Knt. m . . . . . and had issue David, and Isabel who m. Thomas Grant or Graunt. (2) Sir David De la Bere 25th Edw. I. & 7 Edw. II., m. . . . and had issue Adam, and a dau. m. John Butler. (3) Adam Delabeare or Delabere, lord of Knolston in Gower, m. and had issue John. (4) Sir John Delabere Knt. 23rd Edw. 3., of Wibley castle, and also owner of a moiety of Marcross, m. Agnes. d. of Sir Payn Turbervill, lord of Coity, and had issue two daughters and coheiresses viz. Elizabeth who m. Sir Oliver St John; and Margaret who m. first Roger Denis and secondly Sir Elias Bassett, knt. Arms: a bend *arg.* cottified *or*, inter 6 martletts of the third. De la Bere of Cheriton. (1) Sir Roger Delabere, Lord of Cheriton and Langenydd, in Gower, about the time of Edward III. m . . . . . and had a son named . . . . . (2) . . . . . Delabere, or Boaer, m. . . . and had a daughter and heiress named Elizabeth. (3) Elizabeth Delabere, m. David Cradoc, who was desc. from

7

Einon ab Collwyn, and had issue Philip. Descendants are Cradocks of Swansea and Cheriton.

[12] King's Remembrancer's Office, Misc. Records, 2 Edward III.

[13] Sir John de Langton, with Sir Robert de Penres, witnessed a Mowbray charter in 1334. He also witnessed a Penrice deed of Edward III, along with the following who are also named here:—Robert de la Mare, Richard Scurlage, Richard Manxel, and Hamon Turbervyle.

[14] The great quantity of plate and armour included 200 platters, worth £351; 100 silver saucers, worth 150 marks; 14 pitchers, 11 dishes, 9 basins, 5 cups, also 23 cups, all of silver; 3 cups of maple, 8 haubergeons for the king's body, 7 haketons, and 2 others worked with a needle with fleur-de-lys, 2 apris of plate gilt, and 4 beds for the wardrobe of the king and his chaplain.

[15] In 1327 Rees Du was alleged to have been concerned with others in assaulting and detaining John le Mareschal at Swansea; and at another time imprisoning and maltreating him at Oystermouth.

[16] William the Hunter had licence of sporting at Pennard, and also freedom from tolls to sell his game throughout Gower from William de Breos.

[17] Robert Mansel, of Oxwich, was probably the son of Henry Mansel, who is said to have settled in Gower in the reign of Edward I. Robert m. Bridget, the daughter of his neighbour, William Langton.

[18] One of the benefactors of St. David's Hospital, Swansea, and witness to its foundation-deed.

[19] John le Wolf, of Swansea (1332) son of Richard le Wolf, had for his seal (appended to a power of attorney dated 20 November, 6 Edward III.) a rose or six-foil, on it a lion's face, and the legend ' En. Mi. Le. Rose. Le. Li (on). Repo (se). (Clark's *Cartae*, 1st ed., Vol. iv., p. 150.)

[20] Mentioned in the inq. of 1319, as to De Breos's alienations of Gower lands.

[21] Philip de Sweneseie. He is also mentioned in the inquisition as to alienations of 1319.

[22] Although this may be Reading, Berks., there was (and is) a Swansea Reding, which in a grant of 1402 (Clark's *Cartae*, 1st ed., Vol. ii., p 59) is referred to as half an acre in 'les redynge de Sweynesey.' There was, much later, a Reeding at Cadoxton-juxta-Neath, a home of the Seys family.

[23] John la Sopere was a witness to the will of Peter de la Bere, made in 1343, 'in my house at Sweynes'.

[24] An early instance of the surname Kneath, which has remained in Swansea and Gower until this day.

[25] Printed at page 319 of Vol. i. of the *Chronicles of Edward I. and II*. (Rolls edition), 1882.

CHAPTER II.

ALINA DE MOWBRAY'S MISRULE IN GOWER. EDWARD III. GRANTS
SWANSEA A CHARTER. JOHN DE MOWBRAY LEADS GOWER MEN TO
BATTLE.-SWANSEA CASTLE RE-CONDITIONED. A VALUABLE HISTORIC
RECORD AND ITS INFLUENCE ON OUR STORY.

An act of parliament had, in the first year of Edward III., restored their
forfeited estates to the families of those who had been engaged in the
quarrel or insurrection of the barons, under Henry, earl of Lancaster, and
had the title of John de Mowbray to the lordship of Gower been clear, his
widow, Alina de Breos, would have come into her inheritance by virtue of
this act. Unfortunately, the wicked negligence of De Breos in completing
his charter, which conveyed the lordship to De Mowbray and Alina,
without obtaining the licence of the king, rendered the gift invalid; but
although the act of parliament did not operate in favour of Alina, the
magnanimity of the king was graciously extended to her, and in the same
year the gift was legalised by charter, and confirmed in her favour, the
exchequer being enriched thereby to the extent of 100 shillings. The
charter is dated at York, 1st March, 1327. [1]

Alina de Mowbray married again, but at what date we do not know. On
28 October, 1328, according to the patent roll, there was granted to Roger
de Swynnerton (constable of the Tower, and at this time in close
attendance upon the king) 'what pertains to the king of the marriage[2] of
Alina, late the wife of John de Mowbray, tenant in chief.' So that her
marriage must have taken place subsequently. On the previous 9th May,
the king had confirmed, for a fine of 40s., a grant by Alina de Mowbray,
'mother of John de Mowbray,' to Richard de Peshale, for the term of her
life, of manors in Bedford, Northants, and Warwick. It was this Sir Richard
de Peshale, knight, who became her second husband. We have already met
him as the principal commissioner appointed by Edward III. to enquire
into the misappropriation of the goods of the unfortunate Edward II. at
Swansea. He was probably one of the king's justiciars in South Wales, and,
from the frequency with which his name appears, must have been a man
of many activities.[3]

In 1331 Sir Richard de Peshale and Alina were involved in law-suits with
their tenants and men of Gower. In the patent roll of the year is recorded a
commission dated 26th January, issued to Roger Chaundos, John Inge,[4]
Hugh de Langelond, and Adam Lucas, on the petition of Gilbert de
Turbervill, to cause to be brought before them and examined, the record
and process of a plea by the latter against De Peshale and his wife, in their
court of Gower, to recover the manor of Landimor, which Morgan Chan

9

(Gam) gave 'after the custom of these parts, in free marriage with Matilda his daughter,' to Gilbert de Turbervill, and which, after the death of Gilbert, Matilda, Richard their son, and Payne, son of the last named, ought to have come to the petitioner as son of Payne and heir of the first-named Gilbert and Matilda his wife. Should it be found that justice had been done in the matter by Peshale and his wife, they were not to intermeddle further therein, but if not, they were to proceed with the plea and cause full justice to be done under the laws and customs of these parts. The issue thus raised was not disposed of at this time, but it arose more definitely in 1355-6, as will be seen when we reach that date in our chronology.

Two days later, 28th January, 1331, as appears by the same roll, another commission, in which John Inge was associated with Gilbert Talbot, whom we have already referred to, Ralph Bloyon (or Gloyon) and Richard Penres,[5] was appointed to hear and determine alleged oppressions of the men and tenants of Gower by Richard de Peshale and Alina his wife, by themselves or by their ministers, contrary to the liberties granted by William de Breos to the English and Welsh inhabitants of Gower, or those holding lands in the Englishery there. The attention of the commissioners was directed to the penal clause imposed by De Breos upon his heirs to observe the liberties and customs granted by this charter in two sums of 500 pounds in silver. The jury was to be drawn, if true men could be found, from Gower, otherwise from the men of the county of Kaermerdyn, Cantremawr and Cardygan, and the land of Glamorgan, and the inquiry was to be held 'unless Richard and Alina had done justice therein before the arrival of the commissioners.' Unfortunately we have no record of the proceedings nor of the result of the inquisition.

Alina de Breos died in 1330-1 (5th Edward III.).[6] It is a time-honoured tradition that she was buried in the church of Swansea, which is not improbable, but consequent on the eighteenth century rebuilding no trace of her burial place could be found in the church taken down in 1896. And Thomas Dineley, whose valuable notes made during the visit to Swansea of the first Duke of Beaufort, as lord president of the Marches of Wales, in 1684, are still preserved (*Beaufort Progress*), although noticing other tombs in the church of his day, makes no mention of a tomb of Alina de Breos.

The young John de Mowbray, who now succeeded as lord of Gower, became a favourite of Edward III., who, in the earliest months of his reign (1326-7), gave a practical turn to his friendship by accepting young De Mowbray's homage before he came of full age, and giving him livery of his lands[7] in the shires of Warwick, Northampton, Leicester, and Lincoln, and of his greater estates in Yorkshire; and the young baron immediately joined the king's service and marched off to his wars in Scotland.

In 1329, still before De Mowbray had come of age, and while yet his mother was in possession of the lordship of Gower, Edward III. ordered him to array the men of the lordship against an expected invasion of the French, and the experience which he gained in this effort of administration doubtless helped him in the future, when he seems often to have been called upon for similar duty.

The land of Gower did not pass into De Mowbray's possession until the following year, when his mother, Alina de Breos, died. He then paid £300 fine for the custody of Gower and West Sussex, and De Mowbray was thereafter known as lord of the Isle of Axholme and of the honour of Gower and of Brember.

In the sixth year of his reign (1332) Edward III. granted a charter to Swansea, which, like that of his father of 1312, was an inspeximus, with formal confirmation of the charters of Henry III. and Edward II.; and as the wording of the document is almost word for word with the latter, it would be superfluous to insert it here. The larger part of the great seal, in green wax, still remains attached to the charter, the size of which is about 14 inches by 13. The witnesses are 'the venerable father J., bishop of Winchester, our chancellor; W., bishop of Norwich, our treasurer; John de Eltham, earl of Cornwall, our most dear brother; John de Warren, earl of Surrey; William de Ros de Hamelak; William de Montacute; Ralph de Neville, steward of our household; and others,' and the date is the 18th March, 6th Edw. III. The endorsement, in a later hand, is 'Edward ye 3ds confirmation of Henry ye 3rds charter;' but it should be stated that both the former charters are confirmed.

In 1335 the king, fearing an invasion by the Scots, sent his writs to De Mowbray as lord of Gower, as well as to the lords of other liberties of South Wales, to cause the coast to be closely watched, the men of the lordship armed, and the castles strengthened and furnished; and he also made De Mowbray his lieutenant in carrying out these directions. Two years later (12th February, 1337) De Mowbray and his 'lieutenant' of Gowerland were ordered to assist Bartholomew Burghersh, the king's admiral, in raising provisions and ammunition for the ships then about to sail upon an expedition to France.

In 1341 he received letters from the king (then in Brittany) to make preparations for his wars with France. He was also ordered to prepare 40 men-at-arms and 40 archers for that service, and to be in London on the octave of St. Hilary to settle in council the wages of the soldiers, and he was to array , amongst others, 123 men of his land of Gower for this expedition.

The fear of invasion from the French was at this time very real, and the peninsula of Gower must have been closely guarded in anticipation of such an event. The 'mayor and bailiffs' of Swansea were, in 1342, ordered by the king to make close scrutiny of all who came to the port for a passage, of whom suspicion might be entertained; and to take all letters of credit and others which they considered suspect from them, and send them to the chancery, retaining the bearers, as the king had learned that there were spies upon his coasts in England, and others who sent letters to France and elsewhere to forewarn the king's enemies.

In 1342, De Mowbray attended the king on his expedition to France, and was with him at the siege of Nantz, in Brittany. In the following year another draft was made upon the resources of fighting men in Gower, De Mowbray being ordered to array 150 of them to attend the king on a further voyage to France. This circumstance is the more interesting since we may fairly conclude that, together with his Gower retainers, De Mowbray was present at the battle of Cressy, although his name is not mentioned in Froissart's account of that battle. Welshmen particularly are interested in this notable engagement of the 26th August, 1346, and the men of Gower will always delight in the reminiscence that their forefathers joined with the forces under the Black Prince on that day, when, we are told, Captain Cadwgan Voel desired the Welshmen to put leeks in their helmets, and, when the troops looked about them, they found all to be Welshmen except 130[8].

We find De Mowbray and his henchmen of Gower in frequent demand. Later in the year of Cressy, John de Mowbray was commanded to levy soldiers, and to go with them to fight with him in France; and still again, in the same year, he was ordered to supervise the choosing of Welshmen to fight against the king of France, a later document ordering him to bring 100 men from his lordship of Gower, all to be armed with a pennoned lance or a good bow, which latter was surely an indication that the Welshmen of Gower were still notable on account of their skill in archery.

War-like operations in Scotland and France continued to occupy De Mowbray's attention until 34 Edward III. (1359), and he was on one occasion (1351), whilst chief of the commissioners in Yorkshire for guarding the sea coasts against the still threatened invasion by the French, charged to find 30 men from his lordship of Gower for that service; and in 1358, Lord Neville, who attended the king into France, placed himself in ambush with De Mowbray and other knights, three leagues from Paris, where, Froissart informs us, after a short skirmish the French were defeated.

Amongst the documents which connect this John de Mowbray with the lordship may be cited a deed confirming, in 1334, his grandfather's (Wm. de Breos) gifts and confirmations to Neath Abbey under his Gower charter of 1306, in which he saves to himself and his heirs a red sparrowhawk yearly at Michaelmas, for a tenement in Logherne called 'Ilonde.'[9]

Amongst the charter rolls for 1343 is to be found a mandate issued from Westminster to John de Mowbray, lord of Gower, to be intendent to Edward, prince of Wales, and, although we have no record of De Mowbray's obedience to this command, it raised once more the claim that Gower was subject to the prince's lordship of Carmarthen. The matter, however, came to a head in 1355-6, as we shall see.

In 1350, John de Mowbray confirmed a grant by his grandfather, of 1309, to the abbot and convent of Margam of freedom from toll throughout the land of Gouher for all their merchandise. This latter charter has attached to it a beautiful seal of De Mowbray, charged with a shield bearing a lion rampant for Mowbray, between two wyverns with tails nowy, within a richly-carved Gothic panel, ornamented with ball-flowers along the inner edge, with the latin legend (broken): 'John de Mowbray, lord of Axiholm, Brember, and Gower.'

And in 1352, the manor of Oxinwich and advowson of the church of Oxinwich were settled, in the court of lord John de Mowbray, at Sweynes' on the 5th March, 26 Edward III., upon John, son of Robert de Penres, Johanna his wife, and their heirs, by Richard de la Mare, clerk and William le Ffrenche, chaplain, before Sir Roger de Hewyk', knight, steward of Gouherie, Sir Richard Turberville, John de la Beere, Robert de la Mare, Richard Scurlage, Richard Manxel, Richard de la Beere, and others. It will be observed that at this time the lord's court or chancery had reverted from Oystermouth to Swansea, and it may be considered that the castle here had now been put into some state of repair. Both the former deeds of 1334 and 1350 were dated at Ostremeu.

We have now arrived at an important period in the descent of the lordship of Gower. The Beauchamps (or Bello Campos) had never reconciled themselves to the wrong which they had sustained by being deprived of Gower, and it has already been shown how, in 6 Edward I. (1278), the earl of Warwick of that day, had unsuccessfully entered upon a suit in the King's Bench for recovery of the lordship against William de Breos. About the year 1350 a descendant of this earl, Thomas de Beauchamp, also commenced a suit claiming Swansea and Gower as his inheritance as against John de Mowbray.

By royal writ dated at Westminster 17th October, 26 Edward III. (1352), a copy was prepared out of the Exchequer of the record of the former suit concerning the possession by De Breos of the castle of Swansea and the land of Gower, which set forth all the evidence which had then been adduced. Whether this evidence now prevailed, or whether it was that Thomas de Beauchamp was sufficiently high in the king's favour to constrain his royal master to give him the verdict in his suit, is not clear; let it suffice that he succeeded, and that the castle and lordship of Gower passed once more into the possession of the earls of Warwick.

The patent rolls of 1356 (Edw. III. *Calendar*, Vol. x.) contain a licence for Thomas de Bello Campo, earl of Warwick, to enfeoff Ralph, earl of Stafford, Robert de Herle, knight, and Richard de Piriton, clerk, of the castle of Sweyneseye and the land of Gowher, held in chief, and for them to grant the same to him and Katherine his wife, for life, with successive remainder in tail male; and we are told[10] that, later, De Beauchamp entailed the land of Gower on one of his younger sons.

Although the earl of Warwick had now regained Gower for his family, after long and tedious suits, he found himself almost immediately challenged once more on the score of the lordship being annexed to that of Carmarthen. The claim appears to have arisen out of the gift by prince Llewelyn (*circa* 1217) of Landimor and Kilvey to Morgan Gam (as recorded at Vol. i., p. 232), whose descendants now resurrected this much-hackneyed question.

The appeal was to the Black Prince, and is printed by Clark, who dates it as of 1320. The document is, however, in the sequence of these events, probably 1355-6. It is a breviate of a petition to the crown by the tenants of Landimor and Kilvey, who describe themselves as 'tenants of our lord the prince,' and state that Llewelyn, prince of Wales, gave to Morgan Gam the said lands (of Landimor and Kilvey), 'which were held by the prince as of the lordship of Kermerdyn till John de Breos, then lord of Gower, by duresse and coercion, etc . . . . the earl of Warwick now in seizin of Gower.' They request that the prince's chancery may be instructed to direct his ministers to enquire whether Landimor and Kilvey do not appertain to the lordship of Carmarthen. The grant upon which they based their claim was very brief:—

Know all men, etc., I Llewelyn, prince of North Wales, have granted to Morgan Gam and his heirs all the land of Landymore with its appurtenances to hold by the service of one knight's fee. Also all the land on the east side of the Tawey, as that water falls into the sea. Testibus: Madoc filio Griffith, Maylour Meredith filio Roberti, Ethenwit, Eynon filio Walkeney, Madoc filio Ririd, Maelgon filio Resi Crik, Res filio Griffini.

This claim appears to have quickly matured, and the earl of Warwick, having so recently persuaded the crown to acknowledge his right to the lordship of Gower, now appealed to it to aid him in defending his further claim to hold it as of the crown and not of Carmarthen. The record which arises in this matter, dated 1355-6, is an exceedingly interesting document, and in it the crown sets forth many matters of moment in our local history which have not hitherto been revealed, because, until 1924, the document had not come to light.[11] We have therefore thought it necessary to lay before our readers as brief a précis as possible of a free translation[12] of the document, which is of extraordinary volume, and in Norman-French. It deserves the close attention of the reader.

The earl of Warwick states that he recovered the castle of Swansea and the land of Gower, which William, earl of Warwick, and his ancestors held of the king's progenitors as other barons of the march held their lordships, but that the prince of Wales, at the suggestion of Sir Richard Turbervill and Thomas de Avene, tenants of Gower, claimed that they belonged to his lordship of Carmarthen, and the earl sought the aid of the king and council to defend his right.

To which, answer is made by the crown that the principality of Wales had been granted by the king to the prince and his heirs, kings of England, with reversion to the crown, and it is more advantageous to the crown that the prince rather than the earl should have the royal liberties; also that the land of Gower has been held of Carmarthen from time immemorial, the tenants being attendant there by view of writ until the king granted the liberty to the De Breoses.

The earl urges that he is a peer of the land, and a baron of the march of Wales by virtue of his lordship of Gower, which he recovered in the king's court, to hold with royal jurisdiction and liberties, and he ought not to answer for them at Carmarthen. He is ready to produce evidence of his right, and seeks relief from the impediment he has suffered for more than three years to a damage of £2000.

The crown answers that the land of Gower before the time of King John was a parcel in the services of the honour of Carmarthen, which had been given by King Edward I, to his son, Edward, and his heirs, as head of the principality annexed to that honour; that neither the earl nor any of his ancestors had a chancery in Gower from time immemorial until recently, when he recovered it from the lord of Mowbray, when he made an encroachment to the prejudice of the crown and principality. Regarding the wrongs he alleges he has suffered, he is referred to the prince's court at Carmarthen.

The earl produces evidences of his holding Gower in demesne and in the service of the king in chief as of the crown, and that it has never been held of Carmarthen; and that the manors of Kilvey, Landimor, and Rhossili are within and are held of Gower.

It is answered that the inquest on the plea in parliament said that Swansea and Gower were within Carmarthen and of the body of that county, and had been ever since the kings of England had the lordship of Carmarthen.

The earl states that Roger, his ancestor, conquered Gower against the Welsh enemies of the king, and gave part of the lands to the English who were with him, and established laws at his will, one for the English, still called Englishrie, and one for the Welsh, called Galescherie, and then attorned to the king to hold of him of his crown of England as other barons of the march of that condition did.

After the death of Earl Roger, Gower descended lineally till it came to William, earl of Warwick, who enfranchised his burgesses of Swansea with liberties, granting that they should not be impleaded save in his hundred of Swansea, 'unless anyone be charged with treason against my person or castle,' laying down the process by which they should therefore be convicted in his court; which liberties were still enjoyed. He granted divers other royal liberties to tenants of Gower, which proves that he had royal liberties and jurisdictions, and that neither lord nor tenant was ever intendant at Carmarthen.

Earl Roger also granted the bishops of Llandaff cognizance of all pleas within their manor of Bishopston. The De Breoses and De Mowbrays paid relief at the exchequer for one knight's fee at each voidance, according to the charter made to the former by King John; and at voidances the king's escheator did his office there, and the kings of England had always been seized of the lordship of Gower, except when Hubert de Burgh had John de Breos's service by grant of King Henry.

To which the crown answers, that with regard to things alleged beyond memory no answer is given, and they cannot be tried, but the earl never had royal liberties since the time of memory; that he does not show that the liberties said to have been granted to the burgesses of Swansea were given within memory, and if he wishes to claim that they were so made, the tenants are ready to claim the contrary. At all times within memory lords of Gower and tenants of Swansea have been impleaded by writs of Carmarthen, until after the battle of Evesham William de Breos made an encroachment. The earl has not shown that writs issued from the chancery of his ancestors. The alleged grant to the bishops of Llandaff was before memory, but that they have no liberty from the earl's ancestors is proved by the writs pleaded at Bishopston having to be obtained at Llandaff, the head of the bishopric and outside Gower. Also the bishop holds the manor of the prince.[13] As to reliefs being paid to the exchequer of London, the answer is that the principality was in the hands of the kings to whom they were paid. The earl has not shown that his ancestors paid relief as to the crown and not at Carmarthen.

The earl said that there was evidence of a sheriff holding the country, etc., until 34 Edward I., when Sir William de Breos granted to his English men of Gower that none of his ministers should be made sheriff. The earl's ancestors had enjoyed royal liberties until King John's time, when one of them being under age and in the king's ward, the latter gave Gower to De Breos (4th John).

The answer is that the earl never had a sheriff within memory, and there was no sheriff in Gower until Edward I. granted a liberty to William de Breos, by colour of which he appointed one. Upon protest from the tenants he disavowed the sheriff and his judgments. As to the royal liberties, the earl never had them, as appears by evidence within memory. That Gower was in the wardship of King John, owing to the minority of the earl of Warwick, is disproved 'because in the livery mention was made of the castle of Warwick and not the castle of Swansea;' and in the chancery there was no office of diem clausit extremum of the land of Gower in the time of King John, nor was answer made to the king's exchequer for the issues on account of such minority within memory.

The earl alleges that the lordship of Carmarthen and the land of Gower were both styled honours, and therefore both independent, each held of the king in chief, and neither of the other, nor ever was until Henry III. granted the homage and service of John de Breos to Hubert de Burgh. This was the first time Gower was annexed to Carmarthen, otherwise it would have passed by the first charter with the honours fees, etc., and a writ would therefore have been to De Breos to do attendance upon Hubert, just as writs were sent to Rees Creek, Owen son of Griffith, and Mailgon Vaghan, tenants of Carmarthen.

The answer is that Gower was styled the land of Gower and not the honour, as in King John's charter and the earl's recovery. But if it had been called an honour, that did not prove it could not be held of another honour.

The earl states that since king John's charter the de Breoses had had royal liberties in Gower by the title and in the manner in which the earls of Warwick exercised them since the conquest, and continued to do so from 4th John to 32nd Edward I for over 100 years, when Walter de Pederton, constable of Carmarthen, challenged De Breos's right in parliament, and this Walter and Nicholas de Warwick obtained the warrant and took the inquest of the men of Carmarthen, Haverford, and Cardigan, two years after Edward I. had confirmed the liberties to Sir William de Breos. In Henry III.'s time Morgan Vaghan, son of Morgan Gam,

16

then holding the land of Kilvey, forfeited his land and afterwards procured a charter of pardon from the lord De Breos.

It was answered that in parliament De Breos had claimed to hold the liberty solely by grant of Edward I., waiving any right to hold by grant from King John. William de Breos procured by charter of Edward I. liberties in Gower such as Richard de Clare had in Glamorgan. If the ancestors of the earl had had such liberties in Gower, William would have procured the same. Thus the contrary of what was alleged is proved, and the De Breoses did not take their title from the estate of the earls of Warwick. Three inquests had held that Gower was intendant at Carmarthen. The De Breoses never had a chancery in Gower until after the battle of Evesham, when they made encroachment.

The inquest by Walter de Pederton was taken by men of substance of four counties, a great part of whom were of Pembroke and Hereford, who were not of the lordship of Carmarthen, and although they were not all of the county of Carmarthen, no objections can be raised because the king was a party. As to Morgan Vaughan's alleged forfeiture to De Breos, his ancestors were enfeoffed of Landymore and Kilvey to hold of the prince, as appeared by the charter and by inquests returned, so that he could not forfeit to De Breos, who had no liberty whereby Morgan could be convicted in his court, and as to the pardon De Breos had no power to do this.

The earl says that by the inquest the three cantreds of Strathawy are of the body of the county of Carmarthen; they are Cantremawr, Cantrevaughan, and the third containing the lands of Gower, Kedewelly, and Carnwaltham. Kedewelly and Carnwaltham are not intendant to Carmarthen nor ever were in it. The tenants of Kedewelly pleaded in the court of the duke of Lancaster at Kedewelly by complaint instead of writ, and the tenants of Carnwaltham at Laynthy in Carnwaltham in the same way; and Gower is further from the lordship of Carmarthen than Kedewelly or Carnwaltham.

Answer is made that at each sitting at Carmarthen presentment is made that intendance ought to be done for Kedewelly and Carnwaltham at Carmarthen as well as for Karykenny and Iskenny, 'but the duke, cousin to the prince, has been busy in the war, and so it has been postponed.' Besides their case is different; the earls of Warwick were never seized of a royal liberty.

The earl points to the statement at the inquest that the tenants of Gower and of Swansea, in the time of his ancestors, and whilst the land was in King John's hands, and afterwards in those of the De Breoses, had purchased their writs in the chancery of Carmarthen; and that De Breos had been summoned to the county of Carmarthen at the suit of the tenants of Gower; but this was impossible for, long after the conquest of Gower by the earl's ancestor, Carmarthen was in the hands of the Welsh, and it was incredible that Gower was intendant to Carmarthen, which was in enemies' hands. Nor was it since the conquest of Carmarthen, because the conquest of Gower was earlier, and Carmarthen is not part of the principality. And King John by charter enfeoffed De Breos to hold Gower of him in chief as of his crown for a knight's fee for all services; and that he did suit to the county of Carmarthen was due to the duress of his ministers and contrary to the purport of his charter. the claim of the lords of Carmarthen to jurisdiction in Gower was a usurpation and wrong done to the king.

Answer is made to the contention that Gower had been conquered by the earl of Warwick whilst Carmarthen was in the hands of the Welsh, that 'Henry, son of the empress, founded the priory of Carmarthen before the time of memory, and is found by accord, and the sesin of the said earl is not found of record before the time of memory, nor can it be found earlier by averment, whereby it well appears that the king's estate at Carmarthen was earlier than the estates of the earl.' It is unlikely that an earl would have made a conquest without assistance from his lawful lord, like other barons of the march, who held of Carmarthen; and it is unreasonable that Gower should be different from other lordships.

17

And as far as having the liberty goes it remained with King John, and the earl's ancestors never had it within memory. And although King John enfeoffs William de Breos to hold by one knight's fee for all services, nevertheless he owes suit to the hundred to maintain the peace, and was bound to come by summons to the sessions to be on inquests as are all other lords who hold of the honour, since it is proved before that Gower was held of Carmarthen. As to there being no mention of royal liberties in the grant of Hubert de Burgh, all the royal liberties passed by the grant, and, later, Hubert took the grant of De Breos's services to secure his estates. Although Gower was once independent, it would, by the grant made to Hubert, be held of Carmarthen.

For the earl it is shown that the present John de Mowbray had, on the death of his father, livery made to him by William Trussell, then escheator to the king, and the prince of Wales, when directed to certify the nature of the holding, made return that De Mowbray claims to hold the land of Gower of the king in chief.

To which it is answered that the prince certifies that De Mowbray claims royal liberties under the charter of Edward I., which cannot be taken for evidence.

The earl answers to the contention at the last hearing before the prince and council, that the earl was never seised of Gower or of royal liberties, that it was clear from the plea in parliament between De Breos and De Pederton that De Breos was an intruder, and took for his title the earl's possession of Gower immediately before the land came into the hands of King John.

To which it is answered by the crown that the record does not contain a word which implies that the earl's ancestor was seised immediately before King John's seisin.

The earl claims that the king is seised of his crown of England of the jurisdiction and cognisance of pleas touching the lords of Gower concerning the whole lordship, and he adduces the case of (4 Edward I.) William, earl of Warwick, bringing a writ of right by precipe in chief against Sir William de Breos for Gower; of (16 Edw. II.) a fine levied in the bench between Hugh le Despenser the younger, and his wife, and Elizabeth de Burgh, deforciant of Gower; of (17 Edw. II.) De Breos recovering Gower against Alina de Mowbray and others before justices of assize, the judgment being confirmed in the king's bench; and the present earl recovered Gower by precipe in capite.

The answer is that although the jurisdiction of the king's court has not been challenged, so that Gower appears to be held of the crown, it is not proved that Gower is not held of Carmarthen, for the acquiescence of the parties does not take away the royal jurisdiction of the prince who was not a party; and jurisdictions in the king's court do not confer royal jurisdictions of a chancery upon the earl.

The earl urges that the king's charter of 32 Edw. I. gave De Breos all manner of royal jurisdictions and customs in Gower which Gilbert de Clare had in Glamorgan, which estate passed through the De Breoses and De Mowbrays at all times, and by the charter of Edw. III. to the prince of Wales concerning the principality the services of Gower remained in the crown.

It is answered that when Edward I. granted royal liberties to De Breos, Edward II. was prince of Wales, and lord of the honour of Carmarthen, of which Gower has been at all times held. The grant cannot have taken effect, because the Prince already had Carmarthen with all royal liberties. Again, to the grant made by De Breos, the earl is a complete stranger.

The earl contends, regarding the claim of Sir Robert Turbervill and Thomas de Avene to be tenants of the principality by deed of Llewelyn, and therefore attendant at Carmarthen,

18

that Carmarthen never was possessed by Llewellyn, for although he held the principality until Edward I. conquered it, Carmarthen was a separate entity in the hand of Henry III., who gave it to Hubert de Burgh.

To which it is answered that the lords of the honour of Carmarthen have had royal jurisdiction in Gower as elsewhere in the county of Carmarthen for time immemorial.

For the earl it is stated that, 4 Edw. III., Sir Gilbert de Turbervill, brother to the present Sir Richard, sued on a writ of formedon in the English county of Gower against Sir Richard de Pesale and Alina, his wife, then lord of Gower, demanding of them the manor of Landimor by writ of the same Richard, which begins: 'Richard de Pesale, lord of the honours of Brembre and Gower, to his steward of Gower or his lieutenant, greeting, Command Richard de Pesale, and Alina, his wife, that they justly, etc.' This suit was discontinued owing to the death of Alina, and afterwards Gilbert brought a similar writ against the lord De Mowbray; and he also recovered several lands in the fee of Landimor from his tenants in the same county court as by the rolls plainly appears. Therefore Landimor is held of the lordship of Gower, and is outside the jurisdiction of Carmarthen.

It is answered that Richard de Pesale claimed royal liberty in the right of Alina, his wife, heir of the De Breos by the grant to her ancestor by Edw. I. Again Payn Turberville's writ of formedon in the county court of Carmarthen against William de Breos was put without a day owing to a protection, and was then annulled by Payn's death.

The earl shows that in the charter by which Morgan Gam, ancestor of Thomas de Avene, enfeoffed one Gilbert Turbervill, and Maud, his eldest daughter in the lands of Landimor and Rossilli, the words occur: 'to hold of the chief lord of Sweyn(sea) by the services before due and accustomed,' and Gilbert and Maud did so hold the lands. Also William de Breos, lord of Gower, enfeoffed Morgan Gam by charter, which said: 'to hold of him and his heirs by certain services, etc., before, etc.,' so that the lands are held of Gower.

Answered that Llewelyn, prince of Wales, enfeoffed Morgan Gam to hold of himself by one knight's fee, and a clause in Morgan Gam's charter to Turberville's ancestor that the lands were held of a stranger was unlawful and void. De Breos did not enfeoff Morgan Gam, because he could only confirm a seisin in which he had long before been enfeoffed by the prince.

The earl declares that he had proved by charters that Morgan Gam, ancestor of De Avene, was enfeoffed of the land of Kilveye by Sir John de Breos, lord of Gower, to hold of him and his heirs, and Morgan Gam's heirs so held it until the father of the present Thomas de Avene leased it to him for a term of years, and afterwards quitclaimed to him all his right; and after the recovery by the earl Thomas came to Sweyn(sea) and did intendance and fealty, and had a day to acknowledge his service at the coming of the earl, when he released his right to the earl, who re-granted him possession for his life, when Thomas, planning the disherison of the earl, caused his father to bring an assize against him and the earl and others in the county court of Carmarthen which had no jurisdiction, and caused the assize to pass, contrary to his oath and his deeds.

And to prove that Kilveye was within Gower, Sir John de Avene lately levied a fine in the English county of Gower concerning it, to Thomas his son, and his wife and their heirs.

To this it was answered that the earl never had anything in the lands of Kilveye within memory, and he produced no records in proof of his claim; that Morgan Gam held Kilveye by gift of prince Llewelyn and not be feoffment of John de Breos, who simply confirmed his seisin. Thomas is ready to prove that he never did fealty to the earl. The surrender of Kilveye to the earl was forced upon Thomas de Avene against his will; and the entry of the earl upon the lease held by Thomas from his father was disseisin done to the father, who brought an assize of novel disseisin against the earl in the prince's court at Carmarthen, and recovered possession. As to the fine, the lords of Gower were then claiming to have royal liberty by grant of Edward I., and, by the neglect of the ministers of Carmarthen, the lords of Gower made an encroachment. The charter of Llewelyn is in the keeping of the earl, and he will not give it up.

This voluminous record concludes with the following finding, entered by the crown:—

Thus it is openly proved by divers inquests and records previously put before the council, and also by the grant of the principality made to the father of our lord the king who now is, and by the grant of the principality made to the prince who now is, and by the answers made to the things propounded by the said earl, that no one ought to have the royal liberty except the prince.

The ultimate issue of this much-vexed question of the subjection of Gower to the prince's lordship of Carmarthen is to be found in an entry in the charter rolls (*Calendar*, 34-35 Edward III., Vol. xii.), dated 14th July, 1360, from which it appears that the prince of Wales, 'considering the right of the said earl (Thomas de Bello Campo, earl of Warwick) with the king's assent, by letters patent, for him and his heirs, quit-claimed all the right that he had by reason of the principality of Wales or of his lordship of Kermerdyn, in the lands, liberties, jurisdictions or tenants in the said land of Gower, and the parcels aforesaid' (viz., Kylvey, Landymor, Rossully, and Kitehull). Thus, by the magnanimity of the Prince of Wales was laid at rest another controversy, which had been for a long time a bugbear to successive lords of Gower.

There are some statements in this document, made on behalf of the crown, and therefore apparently conclusive, which lead us to modify deductions we have made in earlier chapters concerning the history of our lordship. At pp. 76-77 (Vol. i.) we have expressed an opinion regarding the conquest of Gower, which appears to need revision after the statements in this document relating thereto; but it must still be evident that there is no direct evidence of a winning by force of arms of the lordship, which would justify the application of the term 'conquest' to its acquirement.

At pp. 172-3 (Vol. i.) we have expressed our incredulity regarding the authenticity of such an event as the sale of Gower, and our arguments against it were concluded by a statement of an expert at the Public Record Office, who at that time was aiding our researches, that no confirmation was to be found in the pipe rolls. This was, unfortunately, an error, and had the testimony of those rolls been forthcoming, our criticism of the *Breviate of Domesday* would have been different.

Mr. C. A. Seyler's clever article upon 'The Early Charters of Swansea and Gower,' written, as the result of a perusal of our work, for the

Archaeologia Cambrensis of December, 1924, defends the correctness of the statement regarding the sale of Gower, and quotes the pipe roll of 30 Henry II. (which we also ought to have observed, since it is referred to in Clark's *Cartae*, p. 1407).[14] The transaction appears to have been of a somewhat triangular character. Bruno the Jew, of London, owed a fine of £1000 to the king (Henry II.), and is ordered to pay it off in part by absolving various of the king's nobles from sums which they owed to the Jews,[15] and the words which are essential to our history are, 'and in quittance the earl of Warwick for the land of Gower, £64.'

The date of this is 1184, which is the year of earl William's death. The transaction is a little unintelligible, but, as Mr. Seyler observes, 'it seems that the king paid off the earl's debts to the Jews (probably incurred for the expenses of his expedition to the Holy Land, where the earl is reported to have died), and took Gower as a pledge. It is mortifying to have to admit our error, but accuracy demands it.

Nevertheless there is this consideration which must arise in reflecting upon any sort of 'sale' of the lordship, that it must have been of quite a tentative character, otherwise subsequent earls of Warwick would not be likely to have claimed, as they did, that the lordship belonged to them; and we know that on more than one occasion they succeeded in establishing their claim. It still seems to us to be improbable that the seigniory could have been sold, and probably the transaction did not amount to more than a mortgage of the rents.

There is, furthermore, only one course of reasoning, it seems to us, which will enable us to follow the succession of the earls of Warwick in relation to the lordship of Gower, so as to account for its being in the hands of the successive kings — Henry II., Richard, and John, after the 'sale' by William, earl of Warwick. We know that earl William died in the Holy Land, but there was no evidence of his death, and an imposter arose who claimed his possessions (Vol. i., p. 177). King Henry would therefore have administered the estates until an heir was found, and Waleran, doubtless, made good his claim to the earldom after much difficulty, but probably never took up seisin of Gower. The King probably insisted upon his doing his military duty for the lordship, and for this reason the earl paid the scutage of £51 3s. 4d. (Vol. i., p. 177) in order to escape that duty in an honourable manner. Richard retained the administration of Gower as Henry had done, and so did John, who, disregarding the rights of the Warwick family, made a gift of the lordship to William de Breos.

NOTES TO CHAPTER II

[1] We are led to believe that the jurisdiction enjoyed in Gower by Alina de Mowbray was not intended to be so extensive as that of her father. Edward III., we know, was anxious to break down the powers of the lords and seigneurs in Wales, and perhaps it was this circumstance that led to a commission of oyer and terminer being issued by petition of the council to Robert de Malle, John Pocock, and Thomas Rose, on complaint by John de Mareschal, that Rees Du, Peter le Cnoyl, Richard le Cnoyl, Hugh le Squyer, William le Cnoyl, Robert le Cnoyl, Robert Dunnyng, Walter Madok, Reginald de Somerton, John Harold, of Sweynese, shipman, the younger, and others, had imprisoned and maltreated him at Sweynese, in the marches of Wales, within the liberty of Alina, late the wife of John de Moubray, of Gower, carried away his goods there, and another time imprisoned and maltreated him at Oystermouth in the same liberty. Dated 13th March, 1327. (*Cal. Pat. Rolls*, Edw. III., 1327-1330, p. 90). During the tenure of the De Breoses in Gower such a commission would have been subversive of the marcher privileges of the lord.

[2] There was much trafficking in the marriages of wealthy ladies, and particularly of widows of 'tenants in chief,' in those days, and probably with much profit to the king. At the same time the right of gift in marriage was often used as security for debt. We have an instance, later on, when, by deed of 16 December, 1502, Sir Mathew Cradock, of Swansea, acquired from Richard Vaughan and Cecill his wife, late the wife of James Basset, and from John Basset, the marrige of Alynor Basset, the d. and heiress of James (and who ultimately married Sir Rice Mansell, of Oxwich). This transaction must be taken in relation to a bond, of the same date, whereby William, Henry, and Thomas Basset secured the performance of covenants to Sir Mathew Cradock.—See Clark's *Cartae* (1910), pp. 1763 and 2384; and also *Genealogies*, p. 349, for relationship.

[3] Dallaway, in *Sussex*, Vol. ii., pt. 2, p. 226, says that amongst the deeds preserved at Magdalen Coll., Oxon., there is 'an order from Richard de Peshall, lord of the house of Brember and Gower, to his bailiffs to pay the tythe of herbage to the Priory of Sele.' Dated 4 January, 1330. 'The seal is very interesting. It appears as if the arms of Braose were borne in an escutcheon of pretence, Richard de Peshell having married Alina, the widow of John de Mowbray, who was heiress of Wm. de Breos.'

[4] John Inge was one of the judges mentioned in the charges against the Despensers drawn up by the barons at their Parliament at Sherburn, near Pontefract, in 1321. The Despensers were said to have, by their influence over the king, appointed corrupt judges ('non sufficienter eruditos'). *Chron. Edward I. and II.*, Stubbs, Vol. ii., p. 68.

[5] On the 24th June in the same year Roger Hillary and Robert de Aston were appointed in the places of Ralph Bloyson and Richard Penres 'in the late commission.' Richard de Penres is referred to in a grant of 1336, in Clark's *Cartae*, p. 1209, as son to Sir John de Penres, knight, and Isabella de Stakepol his wife.

[6] *Vide Close Roll*, 5 Edward III., mem. 6. Mr. Cary Elwes, in his carefully compiled pedigree of the De Breos family, says that Alina died 1360; but in the foundation charter of St. David's Hospital at Swansea, 1332, she is referred to in terms which prove her already dead. The chaplains were to pray for 'the welfare' of the living, and for 'the souls' of the dead, and Alina was included in the category of the latter.

[7] Fines roll, 1 Edw. III., mem. 1.

[8] Rowlands' *Historical Notes* (Cardiff, 1866). The patent rolls (Edw. III., *Calendar*, Vol. vii.) contain a pardon, dated 14 December, 1346, for good service in the war of Scotland, to Philip Syneker, of Swaneshe, in Gower, of the king's suite, for the death of Robert Cartresson, of Gristhwayt, 'fleshwere.'

[9] Reference to 'Ilonde' and the tenure by which it was held is contained in Gabriel Powell's *Survey of Gower*.

[10] Clark's *Cartae* (1910 ed.), Vol. iv., quoting the Rev. H. H. Knight, vicar of Hay.

[11] We owe its discovery to Mr. C. A. Seyler, who explains the circumstances at p. 65 of *Arch. Camb.* for 1924. The roll is filed in the Public Records Office, as roll 9 in the parliamentary and council proceedings, chancery, and is dated 28 and 29 Edward III. (1355-6).

[12] The translation was made for us by Miss Dorothy M. Page, of London, to whom we are indebted for much assistance at the P.R.O.

[13] The manor of Bishopston came again into the field of controversy in 1397 (*Rot. Parl. 520 Rd. II.*). The bishop of Llandaff petitioned Parliament, alleging that through the death of his predecessor Andrew, the temporalities of the see should have appertained to the lord the king during the voidance of the bishopric; but Thomas Beauchamp, earl of Warwick, had entered upon the manor, which lay in the lordship and land of Gower, and thereafter continued in possession and took the profits, claiming that he held the said manor during the voidance by virtue of his lordship of Gower, and he did so in contempt of the king and in derogation of the crown. The bishop therefore entreated the king that the manor and its appurtenances should be seized into the hands of the king and delivered to the now bishop. The petition was granted, and the manor of Bisshopeston ordered to be seized into the king's hands, &c.

[14] In 1362 the king issued his writ of certiorari to discover by what service the ancestors of the east of Warwick, formerly lords of Gower, held that lordship, and the jurors found that William, formerly earl of Warwick, ancestor of the then present earl, held the same by entire barony as the other barons of the marches of Wales held their lordships. (Esch. 35 Edw. III., 2nd pt., 2nd no's., No. 3.) It will be observed that the jury ignored the ownership of Gower by Earl William's successor Walleran, and this gives colour to the statement, to which we have already referred, that William de Newburgh sold the lordship to the king.

[15] The word is 'Jeuws,' Jews, whereas in the transcript used by us it was erroneously written 'Jemos,' the burgesses.

CHAPTER III

MORE ABOUT GOWER ARCHERS. THE BRIEF RULE OF A WARWICK AND THE RETURN OF THE DE MOWBRAYS. A PICTURE OF SWANSEA IN A SETTLEMENT DEED OF 1400. SETTING THE STAGE FOR GLYNDWR'S DESCENT UPON GOWER.

The Thomas de Beauchamp, or Bello Campo, earl of Warwick, who had now become lord of Gower, was made earl marshal of England by Edward III. in 1337, and he was one of the founders of the most noble order of the Garter. He was with Edward III. in the battle of Cressy, fighting side by side with John de Mowbray in the company of the Black Prince in 1346; he was at the siege of Calais in 1347, and at Poictiers on the 19th September, 1356.

The efficiency of the archers from Gower was still held in high estimation by the king. In the patent rolls for 36 Edward III. is an entry dated 15th June, 1362, which commands that, 'because the king had to send without delay no small number of armed men to Ireland, for defence against his Irish enemies,' the sheriff of Gloucester and others named were to 'survey all the archers whom the king had commanded to be arrayed in Gower, to remove such as were inefficient, and send others arrayed in their place, and to imprison contrariants and rebels.'

And on the same date, according to an entry in the close rolls (36 Edw. III., *Calendar*, p. 340), a mandate was sent to Thomas de Bello Campo, 'as he loves the king and his honour, and the safety of Ireland,' to cause forty Welshmen archers of the best of his lordship of Gower, arrayed and furnished, to be taken to Liverpool at the king's wages.

Earl Thomas married Katherine, daughter of Richard Mortimer, earl of March, and died at Calais on the 13th November, 1368. Raphe Brooke's commentator,[1] in his account of the Warwick family, states that, in accordance with the entail already spoken of, Gower passed to Rainburn Beauchamp, the earl's third (and probably second surviving) son. The earl and this son[2] both died in 1368. He also states that on the death of the survivor of them, Swansea Castle and the land of Gower fell to earl Thomas's fifth son, Roger Beauchamp, but the writer gives no authority for this, and the statement is not borne out by the inquisition p.m. of the former earl.

Mr. L. W. Dillwyn in his notes to the Badminton list of lords of Gower, referring to the recovery of Gower by the earl of Warwick, observes: 'I cannot find that the De Mowbray's were actually dispossessed of the lordship, and the litigation between these families was continued until the 20th of Richard II., when the judgment was reversed.' It is, however, evident from the inquisition taken 15th December, 43 Edward III. (1369), upon earl Thomas' death, that he was in possession of the castle of Swansea, the land of Gower, and the manor of Kilvey; that he received rents from Swansea properties, the perquisites of the hundred court, and the pleas of the pie poudre court there, as well as other revenues from Kilvey and Gower.[3]

The inquisition gives us many interesting details regarding the town and lordship.

The jury said that the earl held on the day of his death (Tuesday, 15th December, 1369) the castles of Sweyneseye and Oystermouth, and the land of Gower and its appurtenances by the grant and licence of Ralph, earl of Stafford, Roger Herle, and Richard de Pyrytun, by fine levied in the court of the king in the 30th year of King Edward, between the said earl of Warwick and Katherine, his wife, now deceased, by which fine given and paid to the said earl of Stafford and Robert and Richard, the said earl of Warwick and Katherine, his wife, held the said castle and land of Gower, etc.; and that after the death of the earl and Katherine, the castle and land were to remain to Guy, their son, and his heirs male, and them failing, to Thomas (then twenty-four years of age), brother of the same Guy, and his heirs male. Guy had died without issue.

The jury appraised the value of the castle and land of Gower, but the amount is illegible in the document. Also that there were at Sweyneseye xl. acres of meadow of the value of 4li. per annum; 13s. 4d. in rent of the burgesses of the town of Sweyneseye; a hundred court held there 'de XVa in XVam,' with perquisites valued at 100s. per annum; also a court called 'Placita de Pede pulverisato,'[4] valued at 20s.; also divers rents of tenants of the English as well as of free natives (liberorum nativorum) of 40li. per annum, and an English court (comitatus anglicanus) held from month to month valued at 10li.; and at Oystermouth, two carucates of land, 100s.

Also that the earl held the manor of Kilvye for the term of his life by the grant and delivery of John de Bokyngham, bishop of Lincoln, John de Beauchamp, and others, by fine levied in the court of the king in his 35th year, and that after the death of the said earl, the manor of Kilveye fell to Thomas, his son; that there were there 10li. rents per annum; a certain court held from month to month of the value of 40s. per annum; divers weirs (gurgites) in the water of Tawy of the value per annum of 100s., and so now let at farm; also a certain pit of seacoals (carbonum maritimorum) of the value of 100s., and so now let at farm; also a Welsh court (comitatus) held from month to month, value 10 marks per annum.

There was in Gowaire suprabosco 40li. paid annually in rents; also pasture of the forest of suprabosco valued at 10 marks, now of no value because it is common.

Also a carucate of land at Lanymere (40s.), and two parts of a water mill[5] there (13s. 4d), a court held from month to month (10s.); at Pennarth a carucate of land (20s.), twenty marks in annual rents; a court held 'de tres (tribus) septimanis in tres septimanas;'[6] at Lougherne, annual rents of 8 marks, and a hundred held there twice yearly (20s.); two forests, viz., the forest of Clune and the forest of Kylveye, of no value because common; 'parcus de Bruse' with pasture (100s.); at Sweneseye, two fairs,[7] viz., one at the feast of the Assumption of the blessed Marie and the other at the feast of St. Martin (100s.); at Knyth . . . . . 100s. of rent; one mill at Pennarth (40s.); at Blakepolle a mill (20s.); and finally that the earl held the castles and land of Gower with its appurtenances of the king in capite by military service, and that Thomas de Bello Campo his son, the next heir, was 23 years of age and more.[8]

As referring to earl Thomas's possession of the lordship, we may mention two documents.[9] (1) a grant, which is preserved amongst the

Penrice MSS., by Thomas de Bello Campo, lord of Gower, to Meuric ap Philip and his heirs male of the moiety of a site of a water mill (except the tenth part), which belongs to the said Meuric at Lanrydan, at the Nether Mulne Place, whereof the other parceners are Richard Scurlage and Sir John Beaumond; also land at Lithrid, rent two shillings. Dated at Sweyn' 5th May, 49 Edward III., 1375; (2) a charter by Thomas Beauchamp, earl of Warwick, dated 2nd October, 3 Richard II., 1379, who 'out of our sincere affection in the Lord for our faithful clerk Richard Colet de Sutton, guardian of the hospital of the blessed David at Sweyneseye, and the chaplains and poor persons in the same, and, anxious to secure the continuance of the 'divine service and other works of love' carried on there, ratifies to the said guardian and his successors, and the chaplains, etc., the building and site occupied by the hospital, together with the lands, rents, and services given thereto by Henry de Gower and many other donors; and he conceded to the guardian that he might acquire and possess £20 in church lands or rents within the precincts of the land of Gower, and the same land hold for himself and his successors appropriated to its proper use. This charter is dated at Salwarpe, in Worcestershire.[10]

A few personal details relative to this Thomas de Beauchamp will be of interest, because the circumstances of his life help to explain the restoration of the lordship of Gower, later on, to the De Mowbrays. Just as his father regained possession thereof through his close friendship with King Edward III., so the offence which this earl gave to Richard II. was possibly the reason for the success of De Mowbray's suit against him.

Raphe Brooke[11] tells us how 'this Thomas upbraided Richard II. with the murder of Thomas Duke of Gloucester,[12] his unckle, for which he was euer after hatefull unto him, and so, in the twenty one yeare of the said king's reigne, at a Parliament, he was adjudged and condemned with the earle of Arundell of high treason; the earle of Arundell was beheaded, and this Thomas confined to the custodie of William lord Scroop and earl of Wiltshire into the Isle of Man; a great part of his inheritance, being taken from him, was given to Thomas Holland, earl of Kent and duke of Surrey, halfe brother to King Richard, but after, in the second yeare of King Henry the fourth he was restored againe both to Honour and Lands.'

Lady Warwick,[13] writing in recent years of this Thomas, to whom she alludes as 'patron of Llangeneth Priory' and whom she describes as a man of no striking or impressive individuality, observes that on his dismissal as counsellor of the king, 'he seems, as the vulgar say, to have "taken it lying down." He withdrew to Warwick Castle and lived in retirement there, occupying himself with the building of the nave of St. Mary's Church.'

'The king awaited his opportunity for vengeance, which came in 1397. The earl of Warwick had quarrelled with the earl of Nottingham, who by writ of error, had ousted him from the lands of Gower. Nottingham then denounced him for complicity in a conspiracy, the details of which are very obscure; and King Richard played him a treacherous trick. "He made a great feast," say the annals of his reign, "for the earls of Arundel and Warwick and the duke of Gloucester. Warwick was the ony one who came." The king took his hand, and promised to be his good lord, bidding him not to grieve for the lost lands of Gower; he would provide him with lands of the same value. But when the banquet was ended, he had the earl arrested.' He was committed to the tower — where the name of Beauchamp's Tower preserves the memory of his imprisonment — and brought to trial for high treason.

The dispossession of Warwick of the lordship of Gower by Thomas Mowbray, earl of Nottingham, just referred to, was the result of a writ of error issued, in 1396, to reverse the judgment given in favour of the earl of Warwick in the suit in the previous reign. Richard ordered, on the 12th June, a record of the earlier proceedings to be extracted from the rolls of the pleadings. This was set forth very fully, and included the proceedings in the many previous actions. The record is exceedingly involved, and rendered most obscure by its wearying tautology, and so we forbear to reproduce even the briefest précis of it.[14]

The plaintiff, Thomas de Mowbray, was *persona grata* at court, was earl marshal of England, and in the following year was made duke of Norfolk by the king, so that for this purpose the time was doubly propitious. In prosecuting his suit, he took a strong line of argument which, it is surprising, had not been taken in defending the earlier suit. He alleged that the process upon which it had been commenced was directed to the sheriff of Herefordshire, whereas the lordship of Gower lay in Wales, and therefore the sheriff had no jurisdiction in the matter. Nevertheless, as Dugdale[15] sympathetically observes, 'so fell out the issue of this business, though this error, if it were one, did nothing relate to the just title, that, in 20 Richard II., Mowbray recovered it.' The castle of Swansea and the lordship of Gower came again, therefore, into the possession of this noble family after the lapse of a single generation, and the passing of thirty-six years.[17]

At the same time there is a probability that the suit was not pressed to a verdict of the court, although Dillwyn tells us that the judgment was reversed. The close rolls[18] refer to the discontinuance of the proceedings in the King's Bench in this year (1396), upon a writ of right brought by Thomas de Beauchamp, earl of Warwick, against De Mowbray of Axholme, and records that the former released to Thomas de Mowbray, earl of Nottingham, and marshal of England, the whole of his right to the castle of Swansea and lordship of Gower, as well as to the manor of Kylveye, Landymour, Russelby (Rhosili), and Kythil, etc.

It is remarkable that, high as Thomas de Mowbray [19] had risen in the royal favour, he almost immediately after this period fell into disgrace, and was banished the realm,[20] died broken-hearted in September, 1 Hen. IV. (1399), in Venice, and was buried in the abbey of St. George there. His inquisition post mortem appraised the value of Gower and Kilvey at 700 marks, and it states that 'some time before the day of his death, John Skydmore, escheator and minister of the lord Richard, late king of England, occupied the said castle, lands, manors, and lordships', but by what title the jury was ignorant.

Henry IV, assigned to the widow of this Earl Thomas de Mowbray a third part of the lordship of Gower, by writ dated 20th May, 1400, upon her undertaking not to marry without the king's licence, the custody of the whole of the lordship to remain in the hands of the king[21] until the majority of Thomas, the duke's heir. The assignment of dower was made by the escheater on the following 9th July, and is so full of details of the circumstances of our town at this period, that we are justified in summarising it here.

To the duchess were assigned the county courts of the Englishery, the manor of Pennard, the castle and lordship of Loghere, a third of the lordship of Landymor, a third of a coal-mine (worth 30l. per annum), a third of the forest of Clyn, two mills of Swanesey, one called Brynmell, a fulling-mill, a garden called the Orchard,[22] also the lordship[23] of the burgages underwritten which the tenants hold in Sweynsey:—

John Fairwode[24] holds 2½ burgages in Westestrete, Henry Hatteley, 2½, John Jacob, one, John Fairewode, one, John Horton, 1½, David ap William, the fourth part of one (3d.),[26] Robert ap Thomas, one.

. Seintmarie Strete:—John Horton holds the fourth (3d.) part of one burgage, Jevan ap Cradock,[27] one, Robert Jordan,[28] one, John Wymur, half, Henry Key and Dankyn Ph'ot,[29] the fourth part of one, Thomas ap Ries, half, Robert Jordan, half, Robert Virly, half, William Walmer, 1½, John Williams, half, John Fairewode, one, Jevan ap Cradoc, half, William Taillour, half, Thomas Canon, one, William Williams, one, John Horton, one, Philip Sutton, three (9d) parts of one burgage, Thomas Sengleton, the fourth (3d) of one, John Blake, one, John of Netthe,[30] one, Stephen Wallsche, half, Henry Key, half, John Boner, half, the same John, half, Jevan Kuy (or Kny), the fourth of one, Jevan ap Cradoc, half, Thomas Sengleton, the third of one.

High Street:— Thomas ap Rees, two parts (8d) of one burgage, William Delamare, half, John Baker, Berman, half, William Knoille,[31] half, Thomas Sengleton, half, John Dier, Chaplain, half, Thomas ap Rees, half, Isabella Stackpolle,[32] half, Agnes Doubeney, half, William Dalmare, 1½ burgages, Thomas Sengleton, one, Thomas Milifaunt, half, Philip Stotton, half, John Sair, half, William Dalmare, half, Thomas Meredith, half, Richard Williams, half, Alice Marche, half, Agnes Doudeney, half, John Somery, half, John Dier, chaplain, half, Robert Perkyn, half, Thomas Henry, one, John Seweyn, half . . . . . Heytteley, half, Thomas ap Rees, half, William Williams, half.

Fischeristrete:— Robert Perkyn, one burgage, Thomas Ccrnys, half, Thomas Millifaunt, one, John Horton, half, John Neeth, the fourth of one, Robert Filios, the fourth of one, Philip Hoper, the fourth of one, John Tailour, the fourth of one, David ap Griffith, half, John Horton, one, the same John, half, Henry Poret, one, Henry Key, half, John Horton, the fourth (3d) of one, Ellen (Elena) Key, two parts (8d) of one, Thomas ap Res, one, Richard Richards, half, Cristine (Cristina) Hobbs, one, John Mauncel, half, John Horton, half, Robert Perkyn, one, the same Robert, one, John Touker, visher,[33] half, William Athelard, half, Dankyn Key, half, Henry Key, half, William Bars, half, Richard Mannyn, one, Thomas

Charles, half, Thomas Osbarne, the third (4d) of one, Thomas Sengleton, half, Roger ap llewellyn, one, Walter Williams, half, Jevan ap Henry, one, Ellen (Elena) Key, two parts (8d) of one, Roger ap llewellyn, one, Richard Ricard, half, Thomas Sengleton, one, William Williams, half, Jevan ap Robert, half, Sir John Dier,[34] half, William Dalmare, half, John Fairewode, two.

Yet of High Street:— At the end of the said street on the east side by (juxta) the water of Douereyn,[35] Robert Knepyn and Thomas Malifaunt hold two parts of a burgage, David Fouleyn, the third of one, John Mees, the fourth of one, John Horton, the fourth of one, Thomas Malifaunt, half, of which every burgage yields per annum 12 pence. Sum of the whole rent of burgages, 63s. 5d.

Also assigned to the same a third of the perquisites of the hundred-courts of Sweynesey, a third of the tolls of the chest with censarii-brewing, a weir called Stremeweriss,[36] which Robert Perkyn and John Poket hold, two parcels of pasture called Ilond and Reed-mede,[37] new rent for Robert ap Williams ap Meyrick, for one messuage and 7 acres[38] of land, increase of rent of Felicia Baker for half a burgage, new rent of John Horton for the weir called the Hose, the fourth part of a burgage formerly of Maurice Smythe, a weir which Thomas Seman holds, two Cellars near (juxta) the bridge of the Bailiwick,[39] four 'schoppes' above the said Cellars, two chambers built above the aforesaid 'schoppes' a Garden which Nicholas Harold holds, 20 acres of mountain-meadow (prati montan) at Portmanmede, one void place, formerly of Henry Conewey, which used (solebat) to yield 4 shillings, worth nothing because void and lying waste, one other void place near the forge of Madroc Smyth, worth nothing, one place of land formerly of Thomas Griffith, which used to yield 3d., worth nothing, a weir called Purchasewere and formerly Niewere, which used to yield 16d., worth nothing because void, one pole near Blakestone,[40] which used to yield 20d., nothing now for the cause aforesaid, one burgage formerly of John Trewman, one formerly of John Constable, the fourth of one burgage lying in Stretesend,[41] formerly of Thomas Wrenche, one in Westestrete, formerly of Thomas Taillour, the fourth part of one, formerly of Robert Corow, which said burgage is worth nothing in yearly value because it lies waste, a third part of 8 acres of meadow upon the water of Tawy of no value because of old time (ab antiquo) for the fees of the steward and receiver.

Also certain liberties without the same town by the metes and bounds underwritten, namely:— The whole way which leads from Weststrete[42] of the town aforesaid towards the Skette, and thence towards the Blakepulle on the north side, the water of Blakepulle on the west side, the sea on the south side, and the water of Tawey on the east side.

Sum of the value of the whole dower — £128. 8s. 11½d.

Also assigned to the same in dower the knights' fees under-written, namely:— The manor of Porteynon, which John Penrees holds for one knight's fee, the Manor of Nichollastone and Mauncellisfeld, which Richard Mauncell holds for half a knight's fee, the Manor of Webbeley, which John de la Biere holds by a third part of a knight's fee, also the Manor of Langenythe, which John de la Mare holds of the said John de Penrees, who holds of the lord for one knight's fee, also the Manor of Vorsehull and Vernehull, which John Bounte holds for the fourth part of a knight's fee.

It is worthy of being pointed out here how very few of the burgesses of Swansea, included in this document, bore Welsh names. The Ministers' Accounts relating to the lordship of Gouheria for the year ending Michaelmas 1400 (*Ministers' Accounts* 1202/15) enumerates the various burgages set out in the foregoing document, and there is little variation in the burgesses or the spelling of their names. Amongst the notable dissimilarities are: Walmer in the dower deed and William de la Mare in the minister's account; John Dier and Dieghere; Stackpole and Stackpoell; Doubeney and Daubeney; Stotton and Sutton; John Seweyn and Joan Sweyn; Cornys and Corbeys; John Neeth and John de Neth; Poret and Perot; John Touker, visher, and John Toukere, ffischer; Bars and Bate; Osbarne and Caebern; and Mees and Moris.

The ministers' account contains a considerable extent of property not included in the foregoing document. John de Nethe, reeve of Sweynesey, and Richard Davy, catchpoll there, answer for the farm of the new mill belonging to the king, a fulling mill assigned to the duchess, the farm of the ferry over the water of Tawy, belonging to the king, the mill of westmill, for salmon caught in the tenants' weirs from whom the lord ought to have for each salmon 8d.

The issues of the two corn and malt mills were in the hand of the lord for lack of a farmer, and the two mills stood idle for seven weeks while under repair. The issues of the tolls of the borough chest for the year were 30s. The perquisites of two hundreds at the fairs on the feast of St. Martin and the Assumption of St. Mary amounted to 3s. 2d. And 46 dues of censaria were 15s. 4d. The 'prise of ale' realised £10 16. 10d., from 287 brewings by the burgesses, each of whom would give to the lord for each brewing 14 gallons or 9d. Those who paid dues of brewing gave for each brewing 28 gallons or 18d. The perquisites of the hundred amounted to £11 16s. 8d.

Amongst the 'default of rents' is mentioned that of 'one messuage of Alice March, within the bridge of the bailey of the castle, in the hand of the lord;' whilst the 'costs of the mills' were set forth thus:—

In the stipend of one carpenter for sixteen days making afresh two water wheels of the corn and malt mills, taking by the day 4d., 5s. 4d. And in 29 boards of oak bought for the same work, 3s. 2d. And in the carriage of timber for the same work, 6d. And in 'bordnaill' bought for the same work, 12d. And in repairing the broken spindle of the same mill with part of the iron bought for the same work, 12d. And in two locks with keys bought for the doors of the said two mills, 16d. And in the wages of seven men for six days cleaning the ponds of the said two mills, to each by the day 3d., 10s. 6d. And in one wooden 'hoop' bought for measuring in the mills there, 6d. Sum, 23s. 6d.

In the years intervening between the inquisition of 1369 and the proceedings for recovery of Gower by Thomas de Mowbray in 1396, there is evidence of the castle of Swansea having fallen into neglect. Its bailey was given up either wholly or in part to prominent tenants of the lord, amongst whom were John de Penres, lord of Oxwich, and Sir John de la Bere. Whether the duty of castle guard which was due from them, as from other manors in Gower, entitled them to possess burgages in the castle bailey, and to transmit them to others, we do not know.

It is certain that this was the case at Cardiff. Sir Edward Mansell, of Margam, writing in 1591 *An Account of the cause of the Conquest of Glamorgan by Sir Robert Fitz Hamon and his Twelve Knights,*says:—

The lord dwelt himself most in the said castle or town of Cardyf, being a fair haven town. And because he would have the aforesaid twelve knights and their heirs give evidence upon him every county day (which was always kept by the sheriff in the upper ward of the said castle on the Monday monthly as is before said), he gave every one of them a lodging within the said upper ward, the which their heirs, or those that purchased the same of their heirs, do enjoy at this day.

And Mr. G. T. Clark[43] quotes the patent rolls to shew that, in 1208, King John called on the barons and knights of the honour of Glamorgan and of the honour of Cardiff, to put in repair his houses in the ballium of the castle, as they were wont to do, so that they might discharge their castle guards as they valued their fees. And he continues, 'This shows that the greater tenants occupied houses in the castle court, which were kept in repair by them, though belonging to the lord.' This differs somewhat from Sir Edw. Mansell's statement, but serves to illustrate our point that the chief tenants of Gower held houses and land within the bailey of Swansea Castle. But in the middle of the 14th century they appear to have leased them to others; an indication that the strength of the fortress had already departed.

Even as early as 1324 we find space in the outer bailey of the castle being alienated from its proper purpose by a deed which we have already quoted, whereby John Pistor, of Penmaen, disposed of a piece of land lying in the outer bailey. There were burgages in the castle bailey[44] also, which form the subject of three leases or grants in the 7 and 8 Richard II. (1383-4). Their descriptions were:

(1) John de Penres, lord of Oxwich, granted to John (sometimes called Jenkin or Jankin) Horton and Margaret, his wife, of Swansea, 'a place burgage lying in the bailey of the castle between the garden of John de Horton on the west, and the common road on the east, and the land against the bailey wall on the north, and the tenement of the said John on the south parts;' the rent, a rose flower at the Nativity of St. John the Baptist.

(2) John de Horton,[45] of Swansea, granted to John de Penres, lord of Oxwich, a place burgage, which he had by feoffment of Sir John de la Bere, knight, in the castle bailey, between the grange, formerly John Phillips's, on the west, and the tenement of Robert Ffilias on the east, to be held by John de Penres, for his heirs and assigns for ever, of the chief lord of Swansea by rent and service to be paid to him, and of legal custom.

(3) John, son of Sir John de la Bere, knight, quit-claimed to John de Penres, lord of Oxwich, a place burgage in the castle bailey between the land of Robert Ffilias on the east, and the land once belonging to John Philip on the west. The witnesses to this last deed are interesting people: Robert ap Thomas, vice comite of Gouherie, William Mathew, preposito of Swansea, Thomas de Singleton, Robert Kenepyn, Thomas Charles, Thomas Bortheward, and others.[46]

In addition to these leasings and disposals of sites within the castle bailey, we must remember that portions of the castle itself, particularly some of its towers, had been mentioned amongst his possessions which were alienated by William de Breos and his ancestors, as indicated in the record of the inquisition of 1319; and as we have no information regarding the reconveyance to the lord of this alienated property, we may presume that the grantees entered into possession, and used their property for domestic or trade purposes. We can thus understand how as a fortress the castle of Swansea had at this time fallen, if not into disuse, at any rate into a condition such as would offer but little defence against a determined assault, such as that to which it was soon to be subjected by the adherents of Owen Glyndwr.

In 1399 King Richard II. was at Swansea, en route, with his unfortunate expedition to Ireland. According to Sir Thomas Duffus Hardy,[47] the king was at Cardiff on the 8th and 9th of May, at Cowbridge and another place not identified on the 10th, at Margam on the 11th, at Swansea on the 12th and probably also on the 13th, at Carmarthen on the 14th, and he sailed for Ireland on the 29th May.

The patent rolls of the day enable us to be a little more precise, for they prove that the king was at Swansea on the 11th May, and whilst here granted a patent to the burgesses of Chepstowe, giving them the privilege of pontage for five years; and on the following day, the 12th, he was also here, for he signed at Swansea on that day a commission to Henry, earl of Northumberland.

It is to be observed that at this time the lordship of Gower was in King Richard's hands owing to the attainder of Thomas de Mowbray, earl of Nottingham; and taking advantage of this circumstance, Richard, when in difficulties at the end of his reign, prepared to raise money in the lordship.[48]

During the king's stay at Swansea he lodged, most probably, at the castle, and it is probable that the condition of neglect into which, as we shall presently shew, the defences of the fortress had been allowed to fall at this period, extended even to the accommodation within the castle. This was the prevailing condition in neighbouring fortresses also. De Marque, one of the king's courtiers, tells us how the castles 'were totally unfurnished, and Richard had to sleep on straw during his sojourn.' It was the case at Kidwelly, and in the ministers' accounts thereof, payments are recorded for rushes to strew in the apartments of the castle during the king's visit.[49]

[1] *Catalogue of the Nobility.*

[2] Raphe Brooke says that Rainburn was 'dead in anno 43. E. 3.,' so that he probably died before his father, and therefore could not succeed.

[3] There is a reference to this earl's ownership of Gower to be found in the inq. p.m. of Rees ap Gruff knight (no writ preserved, but probably of the 18th May, 30 Edw. III., 1357), who held in South Wales:— 'Keregerwyn, a moiety of the lordship held of Sir James de Audelegh, lord of Lanendevery, by the service of a sparrowhawk or 12d.; and the other moiety held of the earl of Warwick by the same service as parcel of the lordship of Gower: Langiby and Bettous, the barony held for life of the prince in chief, whereof Joan his wife was enffeoffed.'

[4] Pedlar's court, or court of *pie poudre*, held during the fair for the punishment of offences occurring thereat.

[5] This was probably the mill 'at the Nethere Mulne Place' at Lanrydyan, of which Earl Thomas, in 1375, granted in tail male a half of the site with a current of water, to Meurec ap Philip, the other half being then held by Richard Scurlage and Sir John Beaumond.

[6] Probably held in the third week of every month.

[7] *Nundine*, privileged fair at which an arrest could only be made for a debt contracted or promised to be discharged there. (Clark's *Cartae*, p. 1334.)

[8] Clark's *Cartae* (1910), Vol. iv., p. 1325. It will be observed that there is in this inquisition no suggestion of an entail of the lordship upon the younger son by the deceased earl, such as it was stated he had effected; on the contrary, it passed to the eldest surviving son Thomas, now earl of Warwick.

[9] Both these documents are printed in Clarke's *Cartae* (1910), Vol. iv., pp. 1340 and 1346.

[10] It is witnessed by Sir Henry de Arden (who was a follower of the Earl of Warwick, and had a manor in Worcestershire granted him by the earl, 1 Richard II., who was also in a commission to put down Jack Straw and other rebels), Sir Thomas de Byrmyshan (Birmingham), a commissioner of array, and knight of the shire of Worcester, Sir John de la Bere, knight, Richard Scurlage, Richard de Penres, and others.

[11] *Catalogue of the Nobility*, p. 578.

[12] Thomas, duke of Gloucester, was stated to have been smothered 28 Feb., 1367. Another duke of Gloucester, Humphrey Beaufort, was strangled at Bury St. Edmunds in 1447. The latter was for a short period custodian of the lordship of Gower.

[13] *Warwick Castle and its Earls*, Vol. i., p. 104.

[14] There is little that is interesting in the long succession of pleas which is enrolled in the Record Office; but we think it will be useful to reproduce the statement made in those of 1353 (27 Edw. III., roll 14, 132), respecting the vills or manors at the time in the lordship of Gower. John de Mowbray pleaded that the earl of Warwick demanded against him the castle of Sweynesey and the land of Gower, not making the demand in a vill nor in vills as was required by law and ancient custom, when within the land of Gower vills, which the earl might have demanded, were the vills of Sweynesey, in which were the castle and 10l. of rent; of Milwodwesketty, with 10 carucates of land; of Ostremuth with the castle and 10 marks of rent; of Thistlebon, with 8 carucates; of Morton, with one carucate; of Kythull, with 3 carucates and a moiety of one knight's fee; of Kilbrogh, with one knight's fee; of Iltwitteston, with one knight's fee and a half; of Pennarth, with the castle, 3 carucates of land, and 2 acres of wood; of Penmayn, with 1½ knight's fees; of Nicolaston, with one knight's fee; of Penrys,

with a castle and 1½ knight's fees; of Oxenwich, with a castle, and 1½ knight's fee; of Reynewardeston, with one knight's fee; of Knoyleston, with one knight's fee; of Porteynon, with a castle and 1½ knight's fees; of Pylton, with a moiety of a knight's fee; of Pavylond, with one knight's fee; of Pitton, with one knight's fee; of Russely, with one knight's fee, of Hentles with one knight's fee; of Langeneth, with 1½ knight's fees; of Lanmadock, with one knight's fee; of Landymore, with a castle and one knight's fee; of Leyshanston, with a castle arid one knight's fee; of Lanndrydian, with one knight's fee; of Louchwarne, with a castle and one knight's fee; of Talband, with a castle and one knight's fee; and of Walterstone, with one knight's fee.

[15] *Baronage*, Vol. i., p. 236. Clark, in his *Cartae*, has printed the pleadings in the earlier suit, as extracted from the Exchequer by order of Richard II.

[16] The De Mowbray who had not been in enjoyment of the lordship of Gower was John, born at Epworth in 1326, who married Elizabeth d. and h. to John Lord Seagrave, by Margaret, d. and sole h. to Thos. Brotherton (whose second wife was Maria, widow of Wm. de Breos, last lord of Gower of his name). He fought much in the French wars, but whilst journeying to the Holy Land was slain by the Turks near Constantinople. His son, another John, recovered possession of Gower.

[17] Leland says, '1397 Thomam comes Nottingham per billam erroris quam tulit contra Thomam Comitem Warwic: recuperavit terras de Gower.'

[18] *Rot. Claus*, 20 Rich. II., p. 2. m. 9.

[19] This earl marshal bore an elaborate coat of arms — per pale, the one of St. Edw. the confessor, and the other of Thomas of Brotherton, and in place of crest, a lion upon a chapeau, with two small collateral escutcheons of Mowbray, compassed about with two ostrich feathers.

[20] The incidents which led to his banishment are told in Holinshed's *Chronicle* in a most graphic manner, and are surrounded with all the glamour of chivalry and romance. The chronicler's account is reprinted in Edw. Parry's *Royal Visits and Progresses to Wales*, 1851, pp. 186-188. There is no doubt that this quarrel between De Mowbray and the earl of Hereford (afterwards King Henry IV.) fomented or precipitated the great feuds which s.
culminated in the Wars of the Roses.

[21] The king appointed Sir Hugh Waterton, knight, to be custodian of Gower, Sir William Stradling being steward of the lordship at the time.

[22] The Orchard. the lord's orchard gave its name to the present Orchard-street.

[23] It is significant that the assignment carries 'the lordship of the burgages.' and not the burgages themselves.

[24] John Fairewode comes into evidence in the ministers' accounts of the next year or two. He was portreeve of Swansea.

[25] John Horton, or de Horton, has already been met with, 17 years previously. He was, in 1383, granted, in tail, the site of a burgage in the bailey of Swansea Castle.

[26] The rent of a whole burgage in Swansea, and generally elsewhere, was 12d.

[27]Jevan ap Cradock was of a notable Swansea family, descended from Einion ap Collwyn. His father was Cradoc ap Ynyr, called 'The Strong,' and his cousin Wenllian married David ap Evan-vwya, from which union came Price of Penllergaer. Jevan, or Evan ap Cradock, is reported to have won the boar's head and sword which was used as the family crest, by the slaughter of a huge wild boar in the forest of Clyne, in Gower, now partly existent in Clyne

valley. His son, Gwilym ap Evan of Gower, m. Gwirvil, d. of Howel Melyn of Upper Gower, and had issue Rees and Richard. Both maintained the name Cradock. Rees's d. and h. Maud Cradock married Sir Hugh Johnys, of Landimore, whose brass is in Swansea church. Richard Cradock m. Jenet, d. and h. of Jenkin Horton of Llandoch, and his eldest son was Sir Mathew Cradock, of Swansea. (See Clark's *Genealogies*, pp. 174-7).

[28] Several of the persons whose names follow, such as Robert Jordan, William Taillour, John Horton , Thomas Sengleton, Robert Filios, Thomas Charles, &c., are familiar as witnesses to local deeds, and as of families long settled in Swansea.

[29] Dankyn is probably Jankyn or Daukyn. Ph' frequently being the contraction of Philip, Ph'ot may be an abbreviation of Philpot, a name which survived in a later century in Swansea.

[30] John de Neeth was reeve of the Borough of Swansea at this time.

[31] Knoille has been already met with, also Cnoyl, in association with Knoilston, or Knelston (see Vol. i. pp. 256-7). We take this opportunity of stating our regret that the church at Knelston, also there referred to, fell, in the winter of 1924-5, into almost complete ruin. The south side with its doorway succumbed first, and then the east end utterly collapsed. Little now remains of the fabric. See Royal Institution of South Wales *Proceedings*, 1924-5 and 1925-6.

[32] Isabella Stackpolle is a name which, either by coincidence or by an instance of longevity, finds its counterpart in a deed of 1336, about 64 years previously (Clark's *Cartae*, 1910 ed., p. 1209), which refers to Sir Robert de Penres, knight, Isabella de Stakepol, his wife, John and Richard his sons, and John his brother.

[33] 'visher' in the next Minister's Account is 'fisher,' an appropriate name in 'fischeristrete.'

[34] The 'sir' indicates his clerkly position; elsewhere in the document he is called 'John Dier, chaplain.' In the next Account 'Dier' is spelt 'Dieghere.'

[35] We are indebted to Mr. C. A. Seyler for the suggestion that 'Douereyn' is 'Dyffryn;' but where 'the water of Duffryn,' in High-street, was, we have failed to ascertain, albeit the indication in the document should be of assistance: 'At the end of the said street on the east side.' Was it utilised to supply the moat of the town walls there?

[36] The names of the weirs in the Tawe are interesting, although at this distance of time there is no clue to the meaning of them. In this document there are named 'Stremeweriss,' 'the Hose,' and 'Purchasewere formerly Niewere,' and we shall later on mention the names of several others comprised in the lordship of Kilvey.

[37] Ilond and Reed-mede. These were adjacent to the Tawe at Hafod. Reed-mede is a more intelligible name than Redmead, or Waun Coch, which at times have been its denomination. The survey of the manor of Millwood, of 1641, refers to 'two parcells of ground, being the lands of the right honourable Henry earl of Worcester, adjoining the river of Tawey holden under the lordship of Gower, and called or known by the serveral names of Morva Coch and the Island, now in the tenure of Charles Jones.'

[38] A messuage and seven acres of land is reminiscent of earl William of Warwick's charter to Sweynesse (see Vol. i., p. 154), wherein seven acres are granted to every burgess with his burgage.

[39] This is the first mention we have of premises which are persistently mentioned in local documents for centuries later: cellars near the bailey bridge, shops above, and, higher still, chambers, or a gallery. The upper-story was long the Town-house, wherein the affairs of the borough were administered. In the Minister's Account for the year ended Michaelmas 1400,

one of these cellars, then vacant, is described as being, 'next the gateway of the bailey of the castle.'

[40] In the earliest maps we have of the river Tawe, 'Blackstone Point' is shewn at the western side of the estuary. The pole near it marked the commencement of the harbour, and dues were collected there, as we have shewn elsewhere.

[41] Stretesend is interesting. Reference is made in this document to the end of High-street.

[42] Weststrete is difficult to recognise. We may refer to it later.

[43] *Land of Morgan*, p. 70.

[44] Col. W. L. Morgan has fallen into a singular error in his well-known *Antiquarian Survey of East Gower* (p. 89) when he observes that: 'The fact was this "bailey" was covered with houses belonging to various owners, and up to the 12th century constituted the town of Swansea.'

[45] John de Horton was of Llandough and of Swansea, and, as his name implies, also of Horton in Gower, and by Margaret his wife had issue Jenet, who married Richard Cradock, the father of Sir Mathew Cradock, who, probably between 1491 and 1497, when he was steward of the lord of Gower, built in this very 'place burgage' the 'place' or manor house, which remained standing until its site was cleared for the building of the south side of Temple-street in 1840.

[46] Clark's *Cartae*, Vol. iv., pp. 1352-3-5.

[47] Intro. to *Close Rolls*, p. xv.

[48] *South Wales and the March*, by W. Rees, 8vo, 1924, p. 66.

[49] Owen's *Little England Beyond Wales*, p. 200.

CHAPTER IV

GLYNDWR'S ADHERENTS DESTROY SWANSEA CASTLE, AND ALL OTHERS IN GOWER. THE PREPARATIONS FOR RESISTING THE ATTACK. THE DANGERS OF PARSIMONY. HOW GOWER WELSHMEN FULFILLED THEIR PROMISE.

In the sequence of our history we have now arrived at that outstanding period marked by the rising of the Welshmen in response to Owen Glyndwr's call to their patriotism. It is needless here to outline, even briefly, the circumstances of that bold attempt to regain for his countrymen the independence which Wales had lost by the extinguishing of the line of Welsh princes, and to regain too all the national characteristics of which they had once been so proud.

We have just referred to the sorry condition of the castles of Swansea and those of South Wales generally at the time of King Richard's visit. The Ministers' Accounts for the year ended 29th September, 2 Henry IV. (1401),[1] preserved in the Public Record Office, enable us to form an idea of the defenceless condition into which Swansea Castle had been allowed to fall. Gates, walls, towers, gaol, and the bailey itself, all were in ruin, so that considerable expenditure was required to put them in order. The reason is not far to seek. The lordship was being administered for the king during the minority of the heir of the deceased earl of Norfolk, and the temporary character of the crown occupation, and the inevitable desire to squeeze from the tenants the uttermost penny, and to cut down to vanishing point expenditure of all kinds,[2] so as to satisfy the claims upon the lordship of the three parties concerned — the king, the duchess Elizabeth, and the young heir — had aroused so much irritation that, in Swansea and Gower at any rate, the moment of Owen Glyndwr's insurrection proved entirely propitious.

The Welsh tenants of Gower, dissatisfied with the hard treatment they were receiving at unsympathetic hands, and their grievances fostering their natural inclinations toward a patriotic revival in favour of a Welsh prince of dominant personality, and against an inconsiderate and unknown English king, rose *en masse* like their Welsh neighbours in Glamorgan. They responded with such enthusiasm that they carried the Norman settlers with them, although the latter played their part so well that they made it appear that they were forced rather to submit to the arms of Glyndwr, than freely take his part; but the effect on Glyndwr's enterprise and on the Gower castles and defences was not disturbed by this qualification.

By royal writ, dated 6th December, 1 Henry IV., 1399, the king had appointed Hugh Waterton, or Sir Hugh de Waterton, knight,[3] to be

37

'seneschal and receiver[4] of the castle and town of Swaynese and the lordship and land of Gower, called Guwersland, and supervisor of all forests, parks, chaces, warrens, and woods within the said lordship and land,' during the minority of the earl of Norfolk. And on the 6th May, 1491, the king appointed, during pleasure, Robert Egerley and John Mathew to audit the particular accounts of all bailiffs and ministers of the castle and town of Sweynse and the lordship 'for levying the arrears beyond the moneys received by Hugh Waterton, the king's receiver.' Waterton's concern was for the two-thirds of the estate which remained after satisfying the dower of the Duchess Elizabeth, and his accounts are full of interesting detail.

The account we shall first refer to shews us incidentally the apparently independent position of the portreeve of Swansea, whose liability to the lord of Gower finished with the payment to him of the farm of the lord's lands and his perquisites arising within the borough. In this account Hugh Waterton answers for £10 1s. 11½d. received of the charge of Thomas Gibbe, portreeve of the borough; and for two sums, £7 and 40s., received from the same Thomas on account of the issues of his office. The only other way in which the borough, apart from the lord's tenants therein, contributed to the lord's income was through Thomas Somora, an official, who paid, in the period of this account, £9 5s. 1d. and £9 13s. 2d. as 'collection of the prise of ale and perquisites of hundreds.' The same Thomas Somora occupied the office of catchpole or beadle of the town, and also janitor or gaoler of the castle, a sorry prison though it were over which he presided, according to this account; and for these offices he was paid by the lord 30s. 4d. annually for the former, and 60s. 8d. for the latter.

ACCOUNT FOR 1400-1

Account of Hugh Waterton, receiver of the issues of the castle and town of Sweynesey and the lordship and land of Gouheria, called Gowersland, etc., from Michaelmas 1 Henry IV., to Michaelmas 2 Henry IV, (1400-1).

Cost of necessaries.—The stipend of two men enclosing hedges around the lord's meadow at Trewydva[6] in gross 2s.; the stipend of divers men felling wood in the forest of Trewydva and carrying it to the river Tawy, with their horses, to the boat, and for the boat carrying it to the port of Sweynesey and thence to the castle,[7] for firewood there for the use of the seneschal, receiver, and other of the lord's ministers staying there this year for inspection on this account, and for taking particulars shewn on this account, etc., 51s., and so much because the seneschal and receiver made their stay within the castle there for the greater part of this year for the safe-keeping of the castle and lordship, because of the rising of Oweyn Glyndourdy, Rees Kethin,[8] and Morgan Kethin, and other rebels and traitors and enemies of the lord king in these parts this year.

38

In cleaning out, digging, and clearing the ditches of the castle and the bailey of the castle, because of the coming of Oweyn Glyndourdo and other enemies rising in rebellion this year, for divers men and labourers hired for this, at task, by a certain contract made, 7s 6d.

Cost of the buildings of the castle.—In divers costs and expenses made for the repair and mending of divers buildings, walls, towers, and other necessary works within the castle, as in stipends of carpenters, tilers, masons, and other labourers hired for this, together with lime and sand bought for the same, 40s. Sum 40s. 4d. (sic).

Cost of Boat of the Ferry.—In mending, and for the greater part building anew the ferry, broken and in ruins in many places, as in stipends of carpenters and other labourers hired for this, together with boards, iron, nails, pitch, stipend of the smith, and other necessaries bought for the same, 22s. 4½d. Total 22s. 4½d.

Cost of Hay.—In mowing, spreading, turning, gathering, and making in cocks, the hay of 8 acres of the demesne meadow at Trewydva, together with the hauling of the same hay from the meadow to the boat, and by boat to Sweynesey, and from the river to the castle, with 4s. for the hire of the boat to carry the hay; 22s 4½d. Sum 22s. 4½d.

Cost of Gaol.—For divers locks, fetters, 'pyrewhittes,'[9] twystes, and iron hooks for hanging the door of the gaol, together with the stipends of divers masons, mending the walls of the gaol in divers places this year, together with sand, lime, and the hauling of stones for doing the said work, 9s. 10d. For one maas[10] of iron and steel, bought anew for the office of the cachpole of the borough this year, 2s. Total 11s. 10d.

Cost of the bailey of the castle and the gate of the bailey.[11]—For building anew, remaking, and mending the walls of the bailey of the castle, broken and thrown to the ground, for the safety of the castle and bailey, because of the coming of Oweyn Glyndourdy, Rees Kethin, Morgan Kethin, and the traitors threatening and rising in these parts to take, burn, and destroy the said castle and town of Sweynesey, and in stipend of divers masons, labourers, and servers hired for this, together with lime, sand, and hauling for doing the said work and carrying, £4 8s. 4d. For two gates at the bailey of the castle, of which one gate was made anew, and the other gate in part mended and repaired by one carpenter hired for this purpose, together with the felling of heavy timber for the same, and hauling from the wood[12] to the castle, together with iron nails, hinges, and hooks brought for the same for hanging the said gates at the bailey of the castle, 66s. 4d. For lead, brought for putting the iron hooks in the walls and making them fast, together with the stipend of one plumber doing the said work, 3s. In mending and remaking the eastern bridge[13] of the bailey leading towards the town, broken down, by one carpenter hired for this at task, together with iron, nails, and other necessaries bought for the same, 7s. 11d. Sum £8 5s. 7d.

Foreign Expences.—In wages of three men-at-arms staying in the castle of Sweynsey for the garrisoning and safe-keeping of the said castle, because of Owen Glyndourdo, Rees·Kethin, Morgan Kethin, chaplain,[14] and other traitors and rebels in their company and army, rising and joining up towards the said parts[15] in the months of September and October this year, as for 28 days, to resist the said traitors and for the safe-keeping of the castle, taking each per diem 1s., £4 4s. 0d. In wages of 18 yeomen archers staying in the said castle for the same cause by day and night, taking each per diem 6d., £12 12s 0d. Sum £16 16s. 0d.

Foreign Expences.—Paid John David, yeoman, going from the town of Sweynsey to London with the letter of William Stradelyng, knight,[16] and seneschal of the lordship of Gower, sent to Hugh de Waterton, knight, keeper of the lands and lordship aforesaid, for divers business touching the government and custody of the said lordship, viz., going, staying there, and returning towards the aforesaid parts, for 14 days, taking per diem 6d., 7s. Paid to the same John going from the town of Sweynsey to Gloucester, in the month of August this year, with a letter of the said William, seneschal to the said Hugh, sent for divers business touching the said lordship, going, staying there, and returning towards the aforesaid parts with a letter of the said Hugh, directed to the said William, for the taking of the lady duchess's dower in the king's hands, for 7 days, taking per diem 6d. for himself and his horse, 3s. 6d.

Paid Robert Braas carrying letter of the seneschal from the town of Sweynsey to Brecknock, directed to the said Hugh, because of Oweyn Glyndourdo and other traitors and rebels rising and joining in the parts of South Wales this year, 2s.

Paid Richard ap Wyllym and David Coppa, carrying letters of the seneschal directed to John Boner and David ap Hopkyn, bailiffs of the said lordship (of Gower), to levy and bring together all the knights, esquires, and yeomen, sufficient to safeguard the said lordship of Gower at the extreme boundaries of the said lordship, because of Oweyn Glyndourdo, Rees Kethyn, and other rebels and enemies of the lord king rising and joining in these parts, 1s. 4d.

Paid Kenwric Smyth and John David, carrying letters of said Wm. Stradelyng, directed to Hugh de Waterton to Kedwelly, for certain causes touching the said lordship, twice this year, 3s. 4d. Sum 17s. 2d.

Expences of the Auditor.—In expences of John Matthew, auditor, and the seneschal and receiver of Gower, and of other ministers of the lord king, staying at Sweynsey to audit and settle the accounts this year, coming, remaining, and returning, for 10 days in October, 20s. Sum 20s.

Carriage of Money.—In expences of the receiver and others with him going from the town of Sweynsey for safe conduct in July and October, carrying £133 6s. 8d., money of the lord king, from Sweynsey to Monemouth and Eton, to deliver the same to Hugh de Waterton, knight, keeper of the lordship. (Sum not stated.)

The remainder of the account refers to matters which do not concern Swansea.

ACCOUNT FOR 1401-2

Particulars of the account of Hugh de Waterton, knight, receiver of the lord the king of two parts of the lordship of Gowher and the town of Sweynesey, from Michaelmas 2 Henry IV. to Michaelmas 3 Henry IV. (29 Sept., 1401, to 29 Sept., 1402), by writ of the king, dated 6 December in his 1st year.

Sweynesey.—11l. 12s. received of Richard Heort, reeve of the town, of the issues of his office; 3s. 2½d. received of the same Richard of the issues of his office; 6l. 8s. 9½d. received of Thomas Somer, cach' of the town, of the issues of his office; 30s. 4d. received of the same Thomas of the issues of his office. Sum 19l. 14s. 4½d.

Welshry in supra bosco.—51l. 13s. 4d. received of Jevan Voya, late bedel of supra bosco of Gower; 32l. 18s. 4d. received of the same Jevan, bedel of this year, of the issues of his office. Sum 84l. 11s. 8d.

Park de Brus.—47s. 4d. received of Richard More, parker there, of the issues of his office. Sum 47s. 4d.

Kiluey.—8l. 2s. ½d. received of Richard ap Jevan Vaughan of his arrears of the preceding year; 31l. 5s. received of the same Richard, bedel there of this year, of the issues of his office. Sum 39l. 6s. 8½d.

Lunon.—48s. 9½d. received of Hoell ap Richard, reeve of Lunon, of his arrears of the preceding year; 21l. 4d. received of Richard Perot, reeve there of this year, of the issues of his office. Sum 23l. 9s. 1½d.

Landymour.—77s. 9d. received of David ap Gruffuth, reeve there, of his arrears of the preceding year; 18l. 12s. 11d. received of the same David, reeve there of this year, of the issues of his office. Sum 22l. 10s. 8d.

Oystremouth.—103s. 6d. received of John ap Gruffuth, reeve there, of his arrears of the preceding year; 29l. 10s. received of William Mathew, reeve there of this year, of the issues of his office; 24s. 8d. received of the same William of the issues of his office. Sum 36l. 2d.

Mine of coals.—46l. 2s. 7d. received of Jevan Lloyd, receiver of the mine of coals, as well as his arrears of the preceding year, as of the issues of his office of the present year. Sum 46l. 2s. 7d.

Trewydva.—62s. 3½d. received of Thomas ap Jevan Vaughan, reaper (messor) there for this year, as well of his arrears of the preceding year, as of the issues of his office of the present year. Sum 62s. 3½d.

Foresters of Gowher.—26s. 8d. received of Jevan ap Gwyllym, forester of Kiluey, of the issues of his office; 51s. received of David ap Hopkyn, forester of supra bosco, of the issues of his office; 9s. 3d. received of Jevan ap Gwyllym, forester of Kyluey, of his arrears. Sum 4l. 6s. 11d.

Welshry of Subbosco.—6l. 17s. 11½d. received of Thomas ap Jevan ap Cradoc, late bedel there, of his arrears; 9l. 6s. 8d. received of Jevan ap Gwyllym ap Rees, bedel there of this year, of the issues of his office. Sum 16l. 4s. 7½d.

Wybbeley.—Of 6l. 13s. 4d. of the farm of the manor of Wybbeley sometime of John de la Bere, chivaler, being in the hand of the king by reason of the minority of John de la Bere, son and heir of the said John, nothing here because the said John proved his age in the county court of the Englishry there, and so was discharged. Sum total of the receipt, 297l. 16s. 5¼d.

Fees and Wages.—Of which he accounts in the fee of Hugh de Waterton, knight, steward of two parts of the lordship of Gowher and the town of Sweynsey, as of two parts of 20l., the whole fee formerly allowed 13l. 6s. 8d., in the fee of the same Hugh in the office of receiver of two parts of the said lordship 6l. 13s. 4d., in the wages of Richard More, parker of Bruz at 2d. a day, 60s. 8d.; in the wages of Thomas Somer, doorkeeper of the gaol there (Sweynsey) at 2d. a day, 60s. 8d.; in the wages of Thomas Somer, catchpole of the town there, for his office as of two parts of 30s. 4d. here allowed by the king, 20s. 2½d., and the residue thereof is allowed by the lady (the duchess of Norfolk), because of her dower; in the fee of John Paty, clerk of the court, and the Welsh hundreds and counties, of as two parts of the said lordship and town yearly, 40s., and so much allowed this year and the preceding year because the said John and the other clerks refused to serve the said office for a smaller fee, as is witnessed by the lieutenant of the steward and receiver present at this account; in the fee of a clerk writing the roll of the account of two parts of the said lordship and town, 20s; in the fee of the auditors for taking the accounts of the ministers of two parts of the lordship of Gowher this year, 40s., by writ of the king of his privy seal, directed to the treasurer and barons of the exchequer, dated 23 May, 4 Henry IV., and enrolled in Easter term, 4 Henry IV., roll 16; and in the fee of the said Hugh, for the office of constable of the said castle for the time of this account, 10l., by the said writ of privy seal directed to the treasurer and barons. Sum 42l. 18s. ½d.

Cost of necessaries.—And in parchment bought for writing the rolls of the court, hundred, counties, (and) the attachments and estreats of the same this year, 14s. 8d., in parchment bought for writing the roll of the accounts of this year, 3s.; in parchment, paper, and ink, bought for writing divers indentures and other memoranda touching the office of receiver, 18d.; in the stipend of two men closing and making anew the hedges round the lord's park at Trewydva, 20d; in the stipend of divers men felling wood and underwood in the forest of Trewydva, and carrying it to the water of Tawy with their horses to the boat, and carrying it

41

by boat to the port of Sweynsey, and thence to the castle to have fire wood therefrom, for the use of the steward, receiver, auditors, and other ministers of the lord there, at their comings this year, 46s. 8d.; and so much this year because the steward and receiver stayed in the castle there for the greater part of this year for the protection of the castle, and the safe and secure keeping of the lordship, by strict command of Thomas Percy, earl of Worcester, lieutenant of the lord the king in the parts of South Wales, because of fear of Oweyn de Glyndourdy, Rees Gethin, and other rebels rising against and annexing the said lordship on many occasions this year; and paid to two men going towards the parts of Melyneth, Buelt, Brekenok, Llannamadeuery, and into divers other parts of South Wales, to spy out concerning the purpose and acts of Oweyn Glyndourdy and other rebels, so that the tenants of the said lordship might be warned and prepared to resist the malice of the same, always fearing their coming, 6s. 8d.; in mowing 8 acr. of the lord's meadow at Trewydva, cutting the grass, and making hay thereof, together with the carriage of the same hay from the said meadow to the boat, and by boat to Sweynesey, and from the water to the castle, with 4s. for hire of a boat, 22s. 4½d.; and in two yards of accounting cloth, bought for the exchequer for the office of the auditors this year, 5s. Sum 101s. 6½d.

Costs of Castle.—And in divers costs and expenses laid out about the repair of divers, houses, walls, towers, and other necessary works in the castle there by mandate[17] of Thomas Percy, earl of Worcester,[18] lieutenant[19] of the lord the king in South Wales, staying there in the month of July this year, as in stipends of carpenters, tilers, masons, plumbers, and other labourers hired for this purpose, together with felling and hauling of great timbers from the forest of Clyne to the castle, the purchase of stone, tiles, lime, sand, laths, and 'lathnayles,' for the same work, as appears by particulars thereof made and examined upon this account, and allowed by the testimony of William Stradelyng,[20] knight, lieutenant of the steward, surveyor of the said works, presented upon this account, which particulars remain among the memoranda of this year, 104s.; and paid to a certain mason hired by piece-work for repairing the walls about the bailey of the castle in divers places this year, 4s.; and in lime (and) sand bought for the same work, with carriage of stone, 3s. 8d. Sum 111s. 8d.

Costs of the passage boat (or ferry boat).—Paid to a certain man repairing the passage boat for three days at 5d. a day, 15d.; in nails, called 'spikenaill,' boards, and pitch for the repair of the same, bought this year, 18d.; and in four ash oars for the said boat, newly bought this year, at 6d. each, 2s. Sum 4s. 9d.

Purchase of Mill-stones.—In 5 mill stones newly bought by the receiver for divers mills of the lord, and by the receiver delivered to divers mills, namely to the mill of Landymour, 2 worth 60s., to the mill of Kylvey 1, worth 30s., to the mill of Cleudauch 1, worth 30s., and to the mill of the town of Sweynsey 1, worth 30s., to be found by the king for the farmers of the said mills by agreement as is testified upon this account, 7l. 10s. Sum 7l. 10s.

Wages of divers men watching and keeping the castle.—In the wages of two men-at-arms and six archers sufficiently arrayed for war, being in the castle there for 28 days at divers times when it was necessary, namely in the months of July and August, about the time of the taking of Edmund de Mortuo Mari,* by order of Thomas Percy, earl of Worcester, lieutenant of the lord the king in South Wales, for safely and surely keeping the garrison, and protection of the castle there on account of fear of the rebels annexing these parts, each man-at-arms taking 12d. a day, and each archer 6d. a day, allowed by letter of the said earl, dated at Sweynsey, the 6th of July, 3 Henry IV., remaining among the memoranda of this year, 7l.; and in wages of four men-at-arms and eight archers sufficiently arrayed for war, being in the castle there for 10 days in the month of October, about the time that Oweyn de Glyndourdy, Edmund de Mortuo Mari, and other rebels were at Brekenok, and there burned, etc., for safely and surely keeping the garrison, and protection of the castle, on account of fear of the said rebels, each man-at-arms taking 12d. a day, and each archer 6d. a day, 4l. Sum 11l.

* Edmund Mortimer

Expenses of the Auditors.— In the expenses of the auditors of the steward, receiver, clerk and other ministers coming to take and determine the accounts of the ministers of the lord the king there this year, together with 13s. 4d. of the expenses of the auditors coming from Rodley, in county Gloucester, to Sweynsey, and returning from Sweynsey to Rodley this year, 50s. Sum 50s.

Foreign liveries.—Delivered to Jevan Lloyd, receiver and keeper of the mine of coals of Kylueye, as in 2884 lbs. of candles, bought to have light therefrom in the pits of coals, to him delivered by 2 tallies, as appears in his account, 21l. 3s. Sum 21l. 3s.

(Two entries here struck out and disallowed.)

Foreign payments.—And paid to Thomas Moubray, son and heir of the earl marchal last deceased, for an annuity of 250 marks, granted to him by the king of the issues of the land and lordship of Gower, at the feast of Christmas, Easter, the Nativity of St. John the Baptist, and St. Michael, by equal portions, namely for the said four terms happening in the whole 3rd year of the present king, namely the time of this account, 166l. 13s 4d., by writ patent of the king under the great seal directed to the occupiers, farmers, receivers, or bailiffs, of the said land and lordship of Gower, dated 22 Dec., 1 Henry IV., remaining in the hands of the said receiver, and by another writ of the king under the said great seal directed to the treasurer and barons of the exchequer, dated 12th June, 2 Henry IV., and enrolled in the memoranda of Trinity term in the same year, roll 6, and by letters of acquittance of the same Thomas delivered upon this account. Sum 166l. 13s. 4d.

Sum total of expenses 26l. 15s. 10d., and he owes by these parcels 36l. 7¼ d. Thereof there are allowed in the engrossed account 35l. 19d. by the said writ of the king under his privy (seal) of the parcels disallowed in the parcels of the account of the last preceding year. And so the sum of expenses in the engrossed account is 296l. 17s. 5d., and he owes 19s. ¼ d.

The remainder of this account is, apparently, lost, and this is as far as the ministers' accounts help us to follow the preparations for the approaching troubles. The account for 2 and 3 Henry IV. (1401 to 29th September, 1402) is the last in the bundle at the Record Office. There are a few other similar records with references to Gower, but not to Swansea, and the bundle containing them is principally devoted to the rest of Glamorganshire. This is most unfortunate, for we are probably robbed of an opportunity of learning when and in what circumstances the revolt reached Swansea, and the manner of the ruin of our castle.

What exactly occurred we do not know, but we may infer from the letter of John Scudamore to John Fairford, presently to be reproduced, that the Welsh people of Gower had declared for Owen Glyndwr, and made themselves responsible for the winning of the castles. The date of the minister's account is much earlier, and it was then believed that attack was imminent. At this early time the inadequate idea of defence was to put an inconsiderable garrison in the castle, 3 men at arms and 18 yeomen archers, and to station the knights, esquires, and yeomen who owed service to the lord in numbers which were thought 'sufficient to safeguard the said lordship' at the extreme boundaries, presumably on the north and west of Gower. If this plan of guarding the safety of the lordship was not

43

subsequently modified, there is no need to speculate upon what occurred, for the enemy within the gates proved a most potent adversary, as we shall see.

We must complete the story of Swansea's fate at the hands of Glyndwr's adherents with the aid of other records, and take up the sequence of events with a hiatus of nine months.

The archdeacon of Hereford, writing from that city on 8th July, 1403, says (his spelling being modernised): 'On Friday last, Caermarthen was taken and burnt, and the castle yielded by Ro. Wydmor; and the Castle Emlyn is yielded; and slain of the town of Caermarthen more than fifty persons. Written in great haste on Sunday, and I cry you mercy and put me in your high grace that I write you so shortly, for by my troth that I owe you it is needful.' He adds, 'I send the copy of a letter which came from John Scydmore this morning.'

The enclosure was dated the previous Thursday (5th July), and addressed to John Fairford, receiver of Brecknock. It is unnecessary to reproduce more than the following:—

'All Carmarthenshire, Kidwelley, Carnwalthan, and Ys Kennen be sworn to Owen yesterday, and he lay last night in the castle of Drosselan, with Rees ap Griffith, and there I was and spake with him upon truce, and prayed of a safe conduct, under this seal, to send home my wife and her mother, and their company, and he would none grant me; and on this day he is about Carmarthen, and there thinketh to abide till he may have the town and castle; and his purpose is hence into Pembrokeshire, for he feels quite sure of all the castles and towns in Kedewelly, Gowerslonde, and Glamorgan, for the same countries have undertaken the sieges of them until they be won.'

The writer of this letter, John Scudamore, had no long time previously been placed in charge of the castle of Swansea, as we have seen by the inquisition post mortem of Thomas Beauchamp, earl of Warwick, of 1397, and was still acting, not as governor or constable, but in the civil capacity of the king's escheator at the time of the earl's death. At the date of this letter (5th July, 1403) Scudamore was custodian of Carreg Cennen Castle, from whence the letter was written, and had held it since the 2nd May, 1402. Two days later (7th July) he was reporting the assault on Dynevor Castle, and from a communication written by its custodian we learn that Owen's force mustered 'eight thousand and twelve score (8240) spears such as they were.'

From this letter, dated 11th July, it would appear that Glyndwr was not then quite so sure that the castles of Kidwelly and Gower would fall into his hands without his personal assistance, for the opening words are: 'I do you to wit that Owen was in purpose to Kidwelley.' It is probable that his intention was to lead the siege of the countries of Kidwelly and Gower, although he was already assured of the enthusiasm of the Welsh

44

inhabitants; but had he done so the work could not have been more effectively completed, as we shall see. His purpose, however, was changed. The baron of Carew, ignorant perhaps of Owen's formerly-expressed design, and not prepared patiently to sit down to await his attack, went out towards St. Clears to meet him, and Owen abandoned his expedition into Gower.

We must not overlook the significance of the closing sentences of Scudamore's letter of the 5th July. Owen 'feels quite sure' of all the castles and town of Kidwelly, Gowerland, and Glamorgan. On 2nd July he had taken Dynevor Castle, on the following day Llandovery, and on the 4th, Llandeilo. Two days later he surprised Carmarthen, slaying fifty of its English inhabitants. But the most striking part of his success at this time was that many strong castles — amongst them Llanstephan, Dryslwyn, Newcastle Emlyn, and Carreg Cennen itself — were betrayed to him by friends in the garrisons. It was, no doubt, for the same reason that Owen 'felt quite sure' of the Gower castles.

The notable Gower family of Penres again distinguished itself at this juncture, and John de Penres was in December, 1403, captured by Owen and remained for a considerable time a prisoner. The patent roll of 4 Henry IV. contains a grant by the king to John Penres, knight, of the castle of Lanstephan,[21] 'in consideration of his good service in capturing it from the Welsh rebels.'

Authorities all agree that Owen's success everywhere, except in Pembrokeshire, was due to disaffection in the garrisons, and to use Professor Oman's[22] words: 'Elsewhere he rode triumphant, and from all the strongholds that still flew St. George's Cross, urgent messages went to King Henry, bidding him come riding night and day with a great army, if he would prevent the whole principality from falling into Owen's hands. But Henry had other business in hand.'

A singularly interesting letter written by the mayor and burgesses of Caerleon to those of Monmouth, in which another letter, from the captain of the town of Kidwelly, is quoted, tells us how, when Owen was in the town of Kairm'then (July 1403), 'he sent after Hopkyn ap Thomas, of Gower, to come and speak with him upon truce; and when Hopkyn came to Owen, he prayed him, inasmuch as he held him master of Brut (*i.e.* a student of the prophecies of Merlyn, and reputed to be himself a prophet), that he should do him to understand how and in what manner it should befal him; and he told him wittily that he should be taken within a brief time; and the taking should be between Kayrmerthen and Gower; and the taking should be under a black banner.[23] He acknowledged that this black banner should decease him, and not that he should be taken under it.'

The letter is printed in Ellis's *Original Letters*,[24] the editor remarking

45

that Henry IV. and Glyndwr were both worked upon by ancient predictions, and each, probably, sought the type of the other in those numerous prophecies which our ancestors, in the 13th, 14th and 15th centuries, were so fond of considering as in a state of progressive accomplishment. The sequel of Glyndwr's history shews that Hopkin ap Thomas of Gower was not infallible as a seer.

Mr. T. Matthews, in his introduction to *Welsh Records in Paris* (1910), tells us that 'assistance from France was slow in coming, but on the Wednesday next after the feast of St. Michael the Archangel (3rd October), 1403, the constable of Kidwelly wrote that Henry Don,[25] and all the rebels of South Wales, with the men of France and Bretagne were coming towards the castle and town of Kidwelly with all their array, etc.' The castle was not taken, although the walls were much battered. Kidwelly must have been held in a state of siege for at least three years, as for that period nearly all relief seems to have been sent there by water.

Swansea, too, at this time was manifestly hard pressed for supplies, but how far it shared the unhappy experience of Kidwelly, which was more adjacent to Owen's headquarters in this region, we do not know. But the position of affairs at Swansea was serious just at this moment, for on the 12th September, 1403, according to the patent roll, the king granted a commission to Peter Courtenay and others to take 20 quarters of wheat, two tuns of wine, eight tuns of ale, 100, 400, and 500 fish, and 20 quarters of oats to the castle and town of Sweynseye; and on the 28th of September, protection was granted for John Zely, of Lanstephan, going with a ship of his to England and Ireland to buy victuals and other necessaries 'for the sustenance of the soldiers and others dwelling in the castle and town of Sweyneseye.'

We have no records of the turbulent times that were now witnessed in Swansea and the whole neighbourhood, and have therefore to gather the data of the incidents which followed from other circumstances. After his work in West Wales had been successfully completed, Glyndwr marched through South Wales. Having been joined in Carmarthen Bay by a small French squadron, he moved in their company into Glamorgan. He had no need to consider Swansea, for it had probably already fallen to the arms of his supporters, so he went on to Cardiff, which he threatened; but the king's troops having been dismissed, Owen retired to his fastness in the hills, only to return in December to Cardiff and lay the town in ruins, save only the house of the Franciscans.

It was in the intervening period, before his first visit to Cardiff, that the destructive work of the Welshmen of Gower was accomplished. The lordship had for long been in the heritage of successive De Mowbrays who were in their minority, and it was thus held by the king, and the castle of

Swansea and the lordship were in the custody of his escheator, or rather his nominee. The insurrection was therefore less restrained than might otherwise have been the case. And there was the almost certain risk of treachery from within the fortress. Anyway there is evidence that the rebels were thorough in their work of destruction.

As we have already seen, the castle had fallen, twenty years or more previously, into some condition of disorganisation. The area of the castle bailey had been transferred to private tenants upon leases, and a more or less general and public approach had been made to the precincts of the fortress, which at once laid it open to easy seizure by a hostile force organized within the town. No doubt full advantage was taken of this circumstance, and the capture and overthrow of the castle was easily effected.

The inquisition post mortem of Thomas de Mowbray, earl of Norfolk, in 1406-7, 'concerning the castle of Swansea and lands of Gower,' makes brief but eloquent reference to the effect of the insurrection. The inquisition was taken consequent upon the death of the earl (who was beheaded at York), and the jury found that the site of the castle was of no value beyond reprises,[26] and they valued the two-thirds part of the lordship and land of Gower and Kylvey, which had belonged to De Mowbray, with all outgoings, etc., 'at 100li. per annum and no more, because, the said lordship and land is now for the great part devastated by the "rebelles Wallensium." '

Three years later a similar inquisition was taken upon the death of Sir John de la Bere,[27] who died seised of the 'fortified manor' of Weobley, held from the bailiff of the escheats of Thomas, formerly earl marshall, son and heir of Thomas, duke of Norfolk, in capite of the king by military service in his castle and lordship of Swaynesey. The jury found that the manor was of no annual value beyond reprises, because the houses and edifice on the site had been destroyed by frequent assaults during the rebellion of the Welsh.

In 1432-3 was taken the inquisition post mortem of John Mowbray, duke of Norfolk. The reference herein to the castle of Swansea is again of the briefest: 'There is in the aforesaid castle of Sweynesey one scite which is worth nothing by the year beyond the reprises of the same;' and precisely similar descriptions are given of the castles of Oystermouth and Pennard,[28] but we have no mention of Loughor Castle, which (according to Powel, p. 170) was razed in 1150, never having been repaired after the battering it received at the hands of Rhys ap Gryffyth, in 1115.

The somewhat negative evidence which we thus possess indicates that Owen Glyndwr's faithful adherents were thorough in their work of destruction, and that the land of Gower, when they had finished with it,

47

retained no sort of military works of defence; and beyond the insignificant strengthening of Swansea Castle at the time of the Civil Wars between king and parliament in the seventeenth century, all the fortresses of Gower were allowed to fall into gradual decay.

As early as 1425, the castle of Swansea had been quite abandoned as a military position, although its offices, such as the shire-hall, where the affairs of the lordship were administered, and the lord's courts, still remained. The bailey of the castle was again thrown open, and a thoroughfare from Wind-street to High-street formed through it. Shops were erected over the castle dungeons, if we may so infer from the inquisition taken after the death of Elizabeth, duchess of Norfolk, in 1425, which describes, amongst the property which she owned, 'one cellar next the bridge of the fortress which is worth by the year 3s. 4d., and four shops above the said cellar which are worth by the year 4s., and two galleries[29] above the said shops which are worth by the year 6s.,' which galleries in later years became the town-house or town-hall, and were situated on the corner of Castle Bailey-street and the Market-place, now Wind-street.

NOTES TO CHAPTER IV

[1] This particular account is to be found in Ministers' Accounts, Bundle 1202, No. 17, in the Public Record office. The account for the previous year is printed, so far as it relates to Gower, in Davies's *West Gower*, Part II.

[2] An instance of this parsimony is found in this very document; the receiver, accounting for 'the fee of John Paty, clerk of the hundred and county courts of the lordship of Gower,' adds that it is 'so much this year because the said John and others, elected to carry out this office, were unwilling to serve for a lesser fee, as is testified by the seneschal and receiver.'

[3] Sir Hugh Waterton is mentioned in the letter from Scudamore to Fairwood of 5th July, 1401, informing the latter that Glyndwr 'felt sure of Gower, etc.,' and asking him to 'write to Sir Hugh Waterton, and to all that ye suppose will take this matter to heart; that they will excite the king hitherward,' etc. Hugh de Waterton, writing to King Henry IV., an undated letter, in 1403, from London, asks to be held excused from approaching the Royal presence, 'by reason of doubt of suffering from taking cold in doing so, which would easily crush me;' in which same letter he reports the rebels as having 'burnt the town of Llandeilo and Newtown (Dynevor), and made a great destruction in those parts in all directions, as far as your lordships of Iskennen and Kidwelly, meeting with no resistance, and were about to have entry to destroy your said lordships, but they were impeded by an inundation, *i.e.*, a storm; and they have also driven the chamberlain of Carmarthen as fas as the town, and have killed some of his men.' And he besought the king that he would immediately send an array of knights and esquires, etc., to protect his honour and punish the rebels. *Trans. Hist. Soc. W. Wales*, Vol. ii., p. 106. It may here be stated that it is not improbable that Henry IV. was in Swansea, for he was at Carmarthen on the 29th September, 1403, and returned immediately afterwards to London.

[4] We are led to believe that Waterton had formerly been seneschal only, the office of receiver having been held by William Langeton. A family of that name was settled at

Kilvrough, in Gower. In the patent of Hugh Waterton's appointment he is called 'the king's knight.'

[5] 'Received of the charge of,' received from his custody.

[6] The lord's meadow was thus referred to in Cromwell's *Gower Survey*, 1650: 'Trewythva, Thomas Jones. A parcell of meadow ground abuttinge upon the river Tawey on the south and east and the freehold of William Thomas on the west, called by the name of Morva'r Arlwydd, val' p. acre, 3s. 2d.; 3li 1s.'

[7] 'To the port of Swansea and thence to the castle.' There was probably no communication between the castle and the river, for, as in the present day, the Strand intervened, and provided an unbroken thoroughfare or right of public way along the side of the river, whose course is now that of the North Dock.

[8] Rees Kethin is mentioned, in the letter from Jankyn Hansard, constable of Dynevor Castle, dated 7th July, 1401, as being with Owen at the taking of Carmarthen.

[9] 'Pyrewhittes' were 'parts to hang a gaol door.'

[10] Maas = mace. In this instance the mace was more than a symbol of authority; a serviceable weapon of iron and steel. It is eloquent of the withering effects of a long peace that there was no armourer or smith in the lord's service who could have made such a weapon; but that one must be bought.

[11] These items, important though the expenses they represent were for putting the castle into a condition of security, fell a victim to the red-tape and officaldom of the period, as did the first of the items under 'Foreign Expenses' which follow, being scored across with the pen, probably in the exchequer, and in the margin taken exception to as 'without warrant.' See note no. 17.

[12] Heavy wood, other than firewood, might be felled in the lord's wood at Clyne, not at Trewydva.

[13] The eastern bailey bridge crossed the castle ditch at about the position of the old Castle Bailey Street, or more probably across the head of Castle Lane. Having passed over the bridge, and arrived within the castle precincts, the bailey lay on the left or west. The 'eastern' presupposes a 'western' bailey bridge; where was it?

[14] Morgan Gethin, chaplain, was doubtless the cleric who, according to the *Episcopal Register* of St. Davids, year 1399, was commanded, under the bishop's privy seal, on 17th January, at Coventry, to 'survey and govern all the lordships, lands, rents, and possessions of the bishop everywhere within his diocese.' In the same year, on the 24th October, Morgan Gethin, who was rector of 'Pencarrek,' was collated to a canonry in the collegiate church of Abergwilli, and the prebend of 'Llansanfred' in the same, vacant by the resignation of Sir Thomas Botiller. There was another Gethin Howel, who was amongst the Welsh scholars in the universities who flocked to Glyndwr's standard in 1400-1. The *Parliamentary Rolls* of Henry IV. (Vol. iii., p. 487) refer to this Howel as 'Howel Kethin, bachiler of the law, duellyng (dwelling) in Myghell Hall, at Oxenford;' and futher record that 'Johan Pole sais that Howel Kethin forsaid shuld have counseilled that Griff ap Jen' sckaier, that duelled undir Breythin, to go till Owen and duel with him, and for to become his man.' Howell was evidently by way of being a recruiting agent for Owen.

[15] 'The said parts,' meaning Gower.

[16] Sir William Stradling was now only deputy steward, apparently, and amongst the witnesses to a Penrice deed of 1400 appears the name of Sir Wm. Berkeley, 'tunc seneschal Gowyre.'

[17] 'By the mandate of.' This authority is not vouchsafed in the account for the previous year with the result given in note no. 11.

[18] Thomas Percy had been made earl of Worcester by Richard II., and accompanied that king on his last visit to Ireland. When the king fled, after his return to Milford, the earl disbanded the army and joined the king's enemies. In 1400, he was made high admiral by Henry IV., and in 1402, his lieutenant in South Wales. In May of that year he was given license to buy 100 bows, 120 sheaves of arrows, and 30 lances, and to take them to South Wales for the furnishing of the castles and fortalices there, without payment of custom or subsidy. In 1402-3, he raised an army at Shrewsbury for the king, but in 1403, he was in the archbishop's plot to overthrow him, and was beheaded 24th July.

[19] His patent as lieutenant of South Wales is dated 31 March, 3 Henry IV. (1402).

[20] Sir William Stradling was of the St. Donat's family, son of Sir Edward, sheriff of Glam., 1367. Sir William went, according to Caradoc of Llancarvan, on pilgrimage to Jerusalem in 1408, and received the order of knight of the Holy Sepulchre, *temp.* Richard II. Sir William held an inquisition 15th June, I Henry IV., at Swansea, as to the relationship between Rd. Mansell and Rd. Scurlage, junior. Ab Iolo's dictum that the Stradlings took the part of Owen Glyndwr appears to be contradicted by the Ministers' Accounts; besides, it is unreasonable to assume that the representative in Swansea of the king, during the minority of the heir to the lordship, should have sided with the enemy.

[21] The Penres family were intimately connected with the castle and lordship or manor of Llanstephan in the 14th century. In 1326-7 (Ministers Account 1220, No. 3) Thomas ap Philip, of Llanstephan, is fined for several defaults against Robert de Penrys.

In 1338, according to his inquisition post mortem, William de Caumpville had, by the king's licence, granted the manor of Llanstephan to his daughters Matilda and Eleanor, who held of the king in chief by service of a knight's fee, and of finding a barded horse or four footmen for any expedition of the king.

Before 1341 Richard de Penres had married Eleanor, and on his death his inquisition post mortem dated 11th March, 1356, shewed him to have inherited the castle and lordship of Llanstephan from his wife, and Robert de Penres, of full age, was his heir. He paid £10 relief in 1357 and took possession of Llanstephan.

In 1367 the king ordered him, on pain of forfeiture, to repair and fortify with victuals and other necessities his castles of Llandestephan and Penrees, 'which are said to be so ruinous and broken down, and left without victuals and armour, that very great peril to the country is likely to result.

According to a Minister's Account (1164, No. 1) the crown had seized the castle and lordship of Llanstephan, 16th June, 1377, by the forfeiture of Robert de Penres, and in 1378 they were granted to Simon de Burley, the Prince of Wales' chamberlain. The forfeiture by Robert de Penres was in consequence of his being convicted (1377) of the killing, on the 4th May, 1370, of Joan, daughter of William ap Lli' at Llanstephan. Subsequently Simon de Burley also forfeited Llanstephan, and in 1391 the king granted to Robert Penres, knight, in consideration of 500 marks, the castle and lordship in as full a manner as Robert de Penres, his father, had previously held them. The authorities for the foregoing succession are quoted at length in the *West Wales Historical Records*, vol. xii., p. 59, etc.

The capture of John de Penres by Owen Glyndwr is referred to in a writ of the king addressed to David Howell (Patent Roll, 5 Henry IV., *Cal.*, p. 331), in which the castle of Llanstephan is stated to be destitute of custody and government on the 19th December, 1403, 'because our beloved and faithful knight, John Penres, later keeper of our castle aforesaid, was lately captured by Owen Glyndwr and other rebels, and is detained up to this', and David Howell was placed in charge during the king's pleasure. The Ministers' Account (1166, No. 1, 1410-11) refers to the death of John Penrys, knt., in 1411, and to his having held

Llanstephan for the term of his life and the association of the family with the lordship now ceased. Further particulars of the Penres family, as lords of Penrice in Gower, are given in Vol. i., p. 103.

[22] *Hist. Eng.*, 1377-1485 (*Political Hist.*, Vol. iv.), 1906, p. 179.

[23] In the indictment of Rhys Griffith (grandson of Sir Rhys ap Thomas), *temp.* H. VIII., it is stated that he was greatly encouraged in his attempt to depose the king in favour of James V. of Scotland, by an old Welsh prophecy, that England should be conquered by a raven and a man with a red hand. It is said that James V. had one of his hands red up to the wrist, and Rhys Griffith (being descended from Urien Rheged) bore for his crest a raven, and it was thought that in these two men the prophecy would be fulfilled.

[24] *Original Letters illustrative of English History*, 2nd Series, 1827, Vol. i., p. 21.

[25] Henry Don was, ten years later, pardoned by the king for his treasonable offences; see *Patent Rolls*, 30th May, 1 Henry V., 1413. And on the 23rd June the king granted to him and his heirs release of all his lands, rents, etc., within the principality of Wales, the duchy of Lancaster, Gowersland, etc., which came into the king's hands because of his rebellion, and are still in the king's hands, to have as he had them before the rebellion.

[26] Reprises were deductions and duties paid out yearly from a manor or lands, as rent, charge, annuities, fees of stewards, etc.—(Cowell).

[27] Sir John de la Bere died 24th September, 1403, and his son Thomas succeeded him as next heir. At the date of the inquisition post mortem the manor of Weobley was occupied by John St. John, as from the date of Sir John de la Bere's death. (Clark's *Cartae*, Vol, iv). We have dealt with the descent of the manor of Weobley in Vol. i., p. 91.

The Office of Works has in recent years done much to preserve Weobley castle from further decay, and the various apartments have been cleared of the modern farmhouse arrangements which had been introduced. These apartments include the solar, on the left of the gateway as you enter the castle, and the vaulted cellars below; the great hall to the east, which was entered from the south-east, and had a fine fireplace and large window at the east end; the hall porch, of great interest; the kitchen block at the north-east angle of the castle; a strong south-east tower now entirely ruined, but with two ovens, a large drain and garderobe shafts in its base; a chapel in the south-east angle of the courtyard, the basement of which was uncovered; and the base of a south-west tower, with an added 14th century gabled building facing westwards. The western gatehouse stands to the height of its parapets, but its south end and the range of buildings are completely ruined. This was the principal entrance to the castle, and was protected by a rock-cut moat which has now been cleared out.

[28] Penard Castle, says Mr. G. T. Clark (*Arch. Camb.*, 1860, p. 299), 'seems to have been a simple inclosed court, with walls from 10ft. to 30ft. high, mural towers, and a gatehouse, but with small permanent accommodation within. The dwellings were chiefly structures of timber placed against the walls, and have, in consequence, long disappeared.'

During the spring and summer of 1927, excavations were undertaken within Pennard Castle by Mr. Percy J. Williams, assisted by Mr. K. S. Meager, and others, and at the western end of the castle enclosure there were uncovered the footings and foundations of a building 40 and more feet long by 27 feet wide. An entrance doorway, exactly facing the main entrance of the castle, was disclosed, the jambs of which are still in position. It would appear, as far as the excavations went, that the apartment was divided into two portions, but further excavations may reveal more. No trace of fire-places, nor hearths, nor of roofing-tiles were discovered, to help to determine what the nature of the building was—probably it was the hall, with a store-room adjoining. As the work of excavation may be continued it is hoped that some further interesting development may be placed on record.

51

[29] It may be worth suggesting that the shops would be penthouses, or lock-ups, built against the bailey wall and over the dungeons; whilst the 'galleries' (wooden structures, which played a very important part in the fortresses previous to the introduction of cannon) evidently remained in their original strength. In warfare the galleries were the platforms from which the defenders cast stones upon the besiegers, this sort of ammunition being raised to its elevated position by means of inclined planes, which were supported by beams inserted in holes in the wall.

CHAPTER V

THE SUCCESSION OF THE DE MOWBRAYS, LORDS OF GOWER. A FUTILE ATTEMPT TO ALIENATE THE LORDSHIP. REMARKABLE CAREER OF SIR HUGH JOHNYS.

Thomas de Mowbray, duke of Norfolk, left amongst other issue by his second wife, Thomas, his son and heir, who was fourteen years old at his father's death. His estates being in the hands of the king, young Thomas seems to have been left to his own resources, and this may easily have accounted for his early offences, attainder, and death.

He was obliged to appeal to the king for assistance, and in his petition dated the 4th December, 1 Henry IV. (1399-1400), he prayed the king to grant him for his maintenance an annual sum out of the lordship of Gower and Kylvey, and also that he might be permitted to remain about the queen's person to learn honour and 'gentilesse,' that he might do better service and pleasure to the king's highness in time to come. The council assented to the petition to the extent of a grant of 350 marks yearly from the lands and lordships until he came of age; and to his brother John they allowed £100 for the maintenance of his estate during the minority of the petitioner.[1] The Gower estates, subject to the duchess's third part, were placed in the hands of custodians: John St. John, chevalier; John Rome, clerk; John Staverton, John Lancaster, Richard fitz Nicholl, and John Lewys, clerk, for whom Thomas Boston, of the county of Northampton, and Nicholas Hall, of Middlesex, were bondsmen, until a surviving heir should reach his majority. The document is dated at Westminster, 30th May, 1403.

Although so young, the earl in the following year joined Roger Scrope, archbishop of York, in his conspiracy against the king, was seized, condemned, and beheaded at York on the 4th June 1404—his head being set up on the walls there, but his body buried within the minster. He bore the title of earl marshal, but not that of duke of Norfolk; and in 1402[2] he had been styled 'dominus de Mowbray, Segrave et de Gower.'

The inquisition post mortem of the late earl was not taken until 1410.[3] It shewed him to have held of his lordship and of fee tail, of the gift of William de Breos to his ancestor, the castle of Sweyneseye and two parts of the lordship and land of Gower and of Kylveye, with reversion of the third part to Elizabeth, duchess of Norfolk, as her allowance for the term of her life. The jury found that the site of the castle of Sweyneseye was of no value beyond reprises, and that the said two parts were valued at 100li. per annum and no more, 'because the lordship and land for the greater part had been devastated by the Welsh rebels.'

There now arises an incident, revealed by the patent roll of 6 Henry IV. (1405), upon which we must place the only construction that is apparent, that, once more in its history, the king attempted to alienate the lordship from the family to whom it rightly belonged, and in trust for whom he held it. At any rate there is not available any other evidence to enlighten us as to what led up to the incident.

The patent roll records a 'grant for life, as much as is in the king's power, to the king's kinsman, Richard Beauchamp,[4] earl of Warwick, of the castle and town of Sweynesey with the lordship of Gower, in South Wales, with all franchises, liberties, royalties, etc., as Thomas Mowbray, late duke of Norfolk, had before the rebellion of the Welsh, the lordship being in the king's hands on account of the forfeiture of Thomas Mowbray, last earl marshal, deceased, son and heir of the said duke; and pardon to him of all sums of money in which his father was condemned by a judgment against him for the said castle and lordship.'

The concluding words of this entry in the roll point to judgment having been entered against Earl Thomas de Beauchamp in 1396 (see page 27 above), and that he had been penalised in costs in regard to the suit between him and the earl of Nottingham concerning Gower. With regard to the grant by Henry IV., referred to in the foregoing extract from the patent roll, it would appear to have had no effect. The lordship does not seem to have passed into the possession of the earl of Warwick, and the probability is that the qualification of the grant in the words, 'as much as is in the king's power,' was an effective demonstration of its impotence.

John de Mowbray was succeeded by his younger brother, Thomas. He was able to prove his age in 1412-13, and had livery of all his estates. He also inherited the reversion of the remaining third part of the lordship and lands which the Duchess Elizabeth had enjoyed until her death. She had married again,[5] after the death of the duke of Norfolk, Sir Robert Gousehill,[6] being her fourth and last husband, and he predeceased her. His inquisition post mortem, taken 5 Henry IV. (1403-4), shows him to have possessed the third part of Gower, etc., by right of his wife, who held it as her 'dotem'; the third part being valued at 200 marks. The Duchess Elizabeth died 3 Henry VI. (1424).

It must be recorded here that on the 26th June, 6 Henry IV. (1405), the king, being then in possession, and lord of Gower owing to the forfeiture of Thomas de Mowbray, granted a confirmation, by inspeximus, of the charter which William de Breos had given to the English and Welsh people of the Englishery of Gower, in 1306.[7] What the circumstances were which led to this confirmation we have not discovered, nor why the confirmation should have been confined to the Gower charter and not extended to that granted to Swansea; at any rate we have found no evidence of the latter charter having been thus confirmed.

After the insurrectionary proceedings of Owen Glyndwr's supporters, Richard Lord Grey of Cudmor was appointed lieutenant and justice of South Wales. His commission[8] was dated 2nd December, 1405, and was accompanied by special letters of intendance to the parts of Gowerland, Kidwelly, etc.

John de Mowbray, who became duke of Norfolk, earl marshal of Nottingham, and lord Segrave and Breos of Gower, served Kings Henry V. and VI. in their wars in France and Normandy, and was almost continuously an absentee from this country, so that his estates were constantly administered by wardens or receivers, under the supervision of his kinsman the king. He died 19th October, 1432, bequeathing, for her lifetime, to Catherine his wife, daughter of Ralph Nevill, earl of Westmorland, the castle and honour of Brember and 'the castle of Gower in Wales,' which was no unusual description of Swansea Castle as representing the lordship of Gower and Kilvey. His widow was subsequently thrice married. Firstly to Thomas Strangeways, secondly to John Viscount Beaumont, and lastly to Sir John Woodville,[10] knight, the queen's fourth brother, who, with his father, Roger Woodville, earl Rivers, was slain at Edgecote, in 1469, in the Wars of the Roses. The duchess's marriage to him in 1465 caused much scandal; an indignant chronicler[11] dubbed it *maritagium diabolicum,* the bride being over 70, the husband only 21. Professor Oman [12] gives the date of the marriage as January, 1465, and says 'the lady was old enough to be the grandmother of the sordid young man, and apparently consented to take him mainly in order to disoblige her relatives.'

It appears certain that the duchess of Norfolk did not retain possession of Gower during her long life, as documents which will be referred to presently will show; and it is possible that she waived her right to Gower in favour of her son, or exchanged it with him for other and more convenient estates, but we have been unable to trace the actual transfer of the property.

This John Mowbray, by deed dated at 'our castle of Sweyneseye,' under the seal [13] of his chancery the 12th November, 5 Henry V. (1417), mortgaged to Roger Joudrell a burgage with its appurtenances in Sweyneseye that lay between the tenement formerly Thomas Gibbe's on the east, the tenement of Richard Horton on the west, and the ditch of the castle bailey on the north, and the king's road on the south parts, [14]rendering therefore the rent, service, and customs as anciently paid and of lawful custom. The witnesses were John St. John, knight, steward there; David ap Hopkyn, locum tenens (lieutenant) there, John Bunt, preposito (or portreve) there; Thomas Malifount, John Soper, John Pacy, and many

55

others.

The Roger Joudrell here referred to is mentioned in 1420 as 'esquire, receiver of the king's kinsman the earl marshal in the parts of Wales called Gowerlonde,' in the patent roll of 7 Henry V. (*Calendar*, p. 263). He had reported to the king that there was such a scarcity of wheat and other corn in Gowerslonde that the people could not make enough bread, and so the men with their wives and children, under the stimulus of hunger, would have to desert that land and go to other parts for bread, or else 'they must eat flesh and other things prohibited to Christians in this sacred time of fasting.' In response to this report, Roger Joudrell was commissioned by the king to buy 200 quarters of beans in the counties of Somerset and Dorset, and take carriage for the same to the port of Bristol, or from Berkeley, and thence to Gowerslonde for the relief of the people there. Rymer's *Foedera* (1717 ed., Vol. iii., p. 88) recites a writ of 1419: 'De Fabis providendis pro pauperibus in Gowerland in Wallia.'

During the absence of the lord of Gower in the service of the king, the latter appears to have made appointments on his behalf, as for instance in the interesting incident of the presentation to the hermitage upon Burry Holms, the small island off the Gower coast at the northern extremity of Rhosilly Bay. From the patent roll (424, 7 Henry VI., part 1, m. 16), under date 27th Novermber, 1429, we extract the following:—

For William Bernard. The king to all to whom, etc., salutation. Know that of our special grace we have granted to our faithful William Bernard the hermitage of 'Sancti Kenyth atte Holmes in Gowerslond,' to have with all the rights and appurtenances thereto belonging, etc. Witness the king at Westminster, xxvij. day of November (1429). By the Council.

And here we may anticipate events a little in order to observe that during the frequent absences of the subsequent lord of Gower, similar appointments were made by the king in council. Thus on the 31st May, 1439, the king at Windsor granted to Thomas Norys 'the hermitage of Holmes in Gowersland, Wales, vacant by the death of Philip, the late hermit;' and in 1442, by privy seal at Westminster, the king granted for life to John Baptist, 'the chapel of Holmes en Gower,' in lieu of a grant thereof to Thomas Norys, surrendered. And much later on, in 1482 (*Pat. Rolls*, 12th March, 22 Edw. IV.), the king granted for life to John Yoroth, chaplain, 'the free chapel called Saynt Keneth and Trinite Well, in the lordship of Gower,' void and in the king's gift by reason of the minority of his son Richard, duke of York, with all its rights and commodities.

The inquisition post mortem of John de Mowbray, dated 11 Henry VI., 1432-3, is interesting. The jury found that he held in his lordship of fee tail the castle of Sweynsey and the land and lordship of Gower and Kylvey, with the members and appurtenances there; and they go on to say that—

There is in the aforesaid castle of Sweynesey one scite, which is worth 10d. by the year beyond reprises. And there is there one borough or town member of the said lordship of Gower, called Sweynesey, in which there are of rents of assize 7li 2s. 2½d. annually . . . . . burgages there at the terms of Easter and Michaelmas equally; and there are there two water mills, called Brynmylles, valued at 60s. per annum beyond reprises; one fulling mill, worth annually beyond reprises, 5s.; one water mill, called Grenemyll, valued annually, 20s.; one orchard of the annual value of 6s.; and there is there a certain ferry over the Tawye of the annual value of 10s.; one meadow, called Iselond and Redmede, annual value, 15s.; and another meadow, called Portaynan-Mede (Portman-mead), annual value, 8s.; three weirs (gurgites) in the water of Tawye, of the annual value of 5s. 4d.; tolls of the Pix there, annual value, 3s. 4d.; and perquisites of fairs there, annual value, 18d.; the 'chesura' there is worth by the year, 12d.; the priceage of beer (profits of brewing) there, annual value, 10li.; and the perquisites of the hundred there, valued per annum at 7li. 8s. 8d.

The inquisition also details the earl's possessions in Gower, referring to a parcel of the lordship called Gawsheria (Welshery) of Supra boscus, where there were annual rents paid by the Welshmen of 40s.; also service rents, 40s., and a certain custom called Gomortha [15] yielding 24s., rents paid in Athelholdene,[16] 6s. 8d., and a member, the castle of Oystremouth, in which was a site valued at 2li. per annum. The jurors also stated that John de Mowbray, duke of Norfolk, was son and next heir, and was of the age of seventeen years completed the 12th September, 1432.

During the minority of John de Mowbray, Humphrey, duke of Gloucester, [17] high chancellor of England, held the 'wardenship' of Gower. He was appointed to the custody of the young duke's estates, 24th November, 1432. For this service he received 500 marks, 'with arrears upon all the lands and possessions which he himself hath to farm of the king during the nonage of John, duke of Norfolk,' and he was to account in the exchequer for the surplus. [18] Evidence of Duke Humphrey's wardenship is found in the writ which he sent, 20th August, 13 Henry VI. (1435), to the coroner of the Englishry of Gower, Hopkin ap Dd. ap Hopkin, to hold at Sweynsee an inquisition after the death of Richard Mansel, of Nicholaston, which was duly taken by the oaths of David ap Thomas ap Jevan ap Cradoc, Resi ap Philip, Resi ap Gwilim ap Jevan ap Cradoc, Henrici ap Jevan ap Cradoc (all these of a notable Swansea family already referred to), Reginald Greno, John Harry de Horton, William Gruffuth of Lamymore, Richard Benet, etc.

The king appointed, on the 14th February, 1433 (*Calendar Pat. Rolls*, 11 Henry VI., p. 254), Geoffrey Don to be steward of all castles, manors, and lands in Gowersland, which were of John, duke of Norfolk, during the minority of the said duke's heir, with the usual fee and wages.

In consequence of his being much of an absentee from this country, the lordship of Gower was again put into wardship in 1448, by virtue of a power of attorney (dated 20th July, 26 Hen. VI.), which the duke executed in favour of William Mathew, esquire, and several others, for the delivery by them of seisin of all his lands of Gower to Humphrey Stafford, first duke of Buckingham.

This John, duke of Norfolk, was the patron of Sir Hugh Johnys, of Swansea and Landimor, of whose eventful, even romantic, career an account is given below, as an appendix to this chapter.

His monumental brass remains in St. Mary's Church, Swansea, and on it the inscription states that Sir Hugh was 'knight Marchall of Ingland under the good John, duke of Norfolk,[19] which John gyave unto hym the mano' of landymo' to hym and to his heyr' for ev'more.' It was doubtless on account of this gift that the inquisition post mortem of this duke of Norfolk makes especial exception from amongst his possessions of the manor of Landimore in Gower.

The duke died 6th November, 1461, and was buried in Thetford Abbey. His inquisition was taken 12th May, 1462, and it was found that the duke had died possessed of 'the castle and manor of Swaynsey, and the land and lordship of Gower and Kylvey, with their appurtenances, except the lordship manor and fee of Landimore and thirty-four acres of arable land, and six of meadow in Oystermouth,' these having been given to Sir Hugh Johnys.

With regard to this gift of Landimor, it does not appear that the licence of the king was received for such an alienation;[20] at any rate, no such licence is now to be found. It is unlikely that, without it, despite the statement on the Johnys brass, the duke of Norfolk could legally give Sir Hugh more than a life interest in Landimore, and as it is certain that the earl of Pembroke, who 'recovered' the lordship of Gower from the duke of Norfolk in 1469, gained Landimore also, it is probable that in the hearing of the suit, the 'gift' to Sir Hugh Johnys was found to be invalid.

APPENDIX TO CHAPTER V

THE CAREER OF SIR HUGH JOHHNYS OF SWANSEA AND LANDMOR

Sir Hugh Johnys, or Hugh ap John, was descended from Maenarch, lord of Brecknock. His father is generally admitted to have been the natural son of Watkin Vaughan, who was the son of Sir Roger Vaughan, who was slain at Agincourt in 1415 (as also was his father-in-law, Sir David Gam). But there is something erroneous about this descent, because it is impossible that Sir Roger could have died in 1415, and that, in 1436, his great-grandson, Sir Hugh, could have been fighting in the east. Sir Hugh Johnys m. Maud, d. of Rees Cradock, and cousin of Sir Mathew Cradock. He bore: arg. a fess gules, betw. 3 cocks crested and jewlapped. Crest, a stag trippant. According to his interesting brass memorial in St. Mary's Church, Swansea, he was made knight of the Holy Sepulchre in Jerusalem, 14th August, 1441, after fighting 5 years in Troy, Greece, and Turkey, under John Palaeologus, emperor of Constantinople. Later, he was knight marshal of France, under John, duke of Somerset (lieut. and capt. general of Aquitain and of the whole realm of France and duchy of

58

Normandy; d. 29th May, 22 Henry VI). And under John, duke of Norfolk, he was knight marshal of England; which John gave him Landimore, in Gower. Sir Hugh desired an alliance in marriage with the beautiful Elizabeth Woodville (afterwards Queen of Edw. IV.), and letters urging his suit, written by Richard, duke of York, and Richard, earl of Warwick, are still preserved in the British Museum. He m. Maud (or Matilda) Cradock before 1460, for in that year there was a grant (Clark *Cartae,* Vol. v.), 'to Hugh John, knight, and Matilda, daughter of Rees, his wife,' of a tenement in 'the street of fishermen,' Swansea. In 1461, Sir Hugh was (1st April and confirmed 25th April) made constable of Oystermouth Castle (*Cal. Pat. Rolls,* 1461-7, p. 81) by his patron, John de Mowbray, duke of Norfolk, who died on the 6th Nov. the same year.

In the patent roll (*Calendar,* 1 Edw. IV., p. 80) there is an insepximus and confirmation, dated 25th Novermber, 1461, to Hugh John, knight, of the following letters patent of the king's kinsman John, late duke of Norfolk, whose possessions were in the king's hands by reason of the minority of John, his son and heir: (1) Grant for life to the said Hugh John, his servant, of the office of constable of the castle of Oystermouth, reeve of the lordship and manor of Oystermouth, and surveyor and approver of all things within the lordship of Gower, with the accustomed fees; a yearly rent of 10 marks from the castle and lordship of Oystermouth, of which the duke hands him 4d. in silver personally in part payment, with power of distraint for arrears; and of 40 acres of his demeane land lying between the town and church of Oystermouth, and between the castle and mountain there, and extending to the sea on the south, for the livery of seisin, of which Res ap William ap Jevan ap Cradock, and Evan ap William ap Evan ap Cradock are appointed attorneys. Dated at Framlingham Castle, 26th February, 29 Henry VI. (2) Grant for life to the said Hugh John and Mary, his wife, of a yearly rent of 20 marks, from his castle, lordship, and fee of Oystermouth, with delivery of 4d. in silver, and power of distraint as above. Dated at Framlingham Castle, 1st April, 29 Henry VI.

Sir Hugh had fought in France, and had been one of the council of Robert Morreys (H. T. Evans' *Wales in the Wars of the Roses,* p. 141). Francis and Bliss, in *Some Account of Sir Hugh Johnys* (1845, p. 7-8), record a 'tryal by combatt' between John Lyalton and Robert Morreys (probably he who has just been named). In this account Sir Hugh appears as 'second' for Lyalton, and also as one of the 'counsel for the defendant Morreys.' In 1463, a quitclaim was granted by Richard Cause to Sir Hugh John and Matilda, his wife, of the tenement already referred to in 'Fischer streete.' Robertsons's *All Souls' College (College Histories,* 8vo., 1899) quotes a draft petition from Warden Kele to Henry VI., compaining 'that Hugh Haddelsey, priest, and Sir Hugth John, knt., taking advantage of the great and inconvenient riots of late fallen within this realm (the Wars of the Roses), have seized on the priory of Llangennith.' This was about 1474. On the 15th Oct., 1485, King Henry VII. notified his receiver of the lordship of Kidwelly, that 'in consideracioun of the good service which Sir Hugh John, knight, did unto us in our tendre age, we have yeven unto hym, by way of reward, the some of ten poundes sterlyng, to be had and perceived, for thees tyme oonly, of the revenous of our seid lordshippe' (*Materials Illustrative of the Reign of Henry VII.,* Vol. i., p. 581). Sir Hugh Johnys had a numerous family, most of whom died young. One daughter m. (according to a MS. pedigree by William Benet, of Penrice Castle, compiled cir. 1609, now in the Royal Inst. of S. W. library) Thomas y Gwyn (son of Jenkin ap Griffith, who m. Phelis vz Ieu'n Dd. Ychan ap Dd. Teg of Gwyn); and a memorandum concerning this daughter, appended to the pedigree, states: 'Willoughby, who dwelled in the castle of Neath, and then ruled the country, passing from the saide castle to the church to heere evening prayer, was slayne by this Thomas y Gwynnes fryndes for suspicion of overmuche familiarity with his wife.' Sir Hugh's fifth child, Gwenllian, m. David Rees ap Jevan, of Ynispenllwch; and his ninth, Jenet, m. John David Morgan, of Cadley and Cefn Gorwedd, Glam. The brass memorial of Sir Hugh Johnys is preserved, albeit somewhat mutilated, in the chancel of St. Mary's Church, Swansea, and a full description of it is to be found in the work by Francis and Bliss, quoted above. In the 12th annual report of the Royal Institution of South Wales is an account of the opening of the grave upon which the brass was originally set up, and the discovery of what was believed to be the remains of Sir Hugh and his wife.

According to Edward Lhwyd's correspondent at Swansea *circa* 1698, Sir Hugh John lived at 'Ye Goedtre' in the parish of Swansea (*Parochalia*, Pt. iii., in *Arch. Camb.*, 1911). Y Goedtre, or Goytre, adjoined Hendrefoilan and Gelli dywill on the west, and lay towards the boundaries of the Swansea and Llanrhidian and Bishopston parishes.

A brother of Sir Hugh was, apparently, David ap John, of Swansea, concerning whom there was revocation of a protection granted to him to stay in the King's service, because he delayed in the city and suburbs of London instead of victualling Calais (*Calendar of Patent Rolls*, 7th Feb., 1464, quoted by H. T. Evans, *Wales in the Wars of the Roses*, p. 141.)

NOTES TO CHAPTER V

[1] *Proceedings and Ordinances of the Privy Council of England*, Vol. i., pub. 1834.

[2] *Court Roll of Dovercourt*, 3 Hen., IV.

[3] Clark's *Cartae*, Vol, iv.

[4] Richard Beauchamp, earl of Warwick, was high in the royal favour. He had been engaged in resisting the rebellion under Owen Glyndwr in South Wales, and, in 1403, captured Glyndwr's banner. Lady Warwick describes him as 'the greatest of all the Warwicks.'

[5] The duke of Norfolk was her second husband. Her first was William de Montacute.

[6] Sir Robert Gousehill was one of the ten knights who were killed on the royal side on the field of Shrewsbury, 22nd July, 1403. He had received the honour of knighthood that morning. (Parry's *Royal Progresses*, p. 238.) By this marriage he had one child, Joan, daughter and heir, who married Sir Thomas Stanley, first Lord Stanley, controller of Hen. VI.'s household, and from them descend the Stanleys of Holt.

[7] The inspeximus is amongst the Penrice and Margam MSS., and is catalogued as No. 391b. (See Birch's *Catalogue* of the MSS., 1st Series, 1893, p. 150.)

[8] *Patent Roll*, 7 Henry IV., p. 50, mem. 30.

[9] Dugdale's *Baronage* (quoting Chichley), Vol. i., pp. 433-5.

[10] It is an interesting circumstance that Sir John Woodville's sister (Mary) was wife of William Herbert, earl of Huntingdon, who became lord of Gower by inheritance from his father, William, earl of Pembroke, who also was slain at Edgecote.

[11] *William of Worcester*, p. 83 (anno. 1465).

[12] *Political Hist. Eng.*, 1906, p. 424.

[13] The seal, in creamy white wax, has on its *obverse*, the earl in armour riding on a caparisoned horse left, on a background replenished with flowers; *reverse*, a large shield, apparently, per pale, *dex.*, a lion rampant, Mowbray; *sin.*, a lion rampant, crowned, Segrave, but only the sinister lion is clear. Supporters, two lions sejant guardant, addorsed, each holding an ostrich feather.

[14] This description of the burgage could only apply to a site in the position of the present Caer-street, on the north side of the Market-place.

[15] Gomortha, from the Welsh Cymhortha, assistance by local contribution. This was forbidden to be levied upon the common people of Wales by statute. 4 Hen. IV., cap. 27.

[16] Rents paid in Athelholdene. 'Three persons who pay an ebidiw of three score pence, a king's talog, an arddelw man, and an alltud, whom the king has enfranchised.' (*Ancient Laws of Wales*, Vol, ii., p. 609.) Athrelman seems to have been a kind of serf, who made a yearly payment to the lord, and whose goods, in case of death without issue, were liable to be taken by the lord.

[17] 'The good Duke Humphrey' died (was murdered it is stated) at his lodging in St. Saviour's Hospital, Bury St. Edmund's, in 1446, and was buried in St. Alban's Abbey.

[18] *Minutes of Privy Council*, 28th Nov., 1433.

[19] On the brass (1462) of 'the venerable Edmund Stapleton, Esquire,' in Ingham Church, Norfolk, he is styled 'chamberlain to the most serene Prince John, duke of Norfolk.'

[20] It is of interest that the *Pat. Rolls* of 8 Rd. II., 1384, shew that Edward le Despenser, late lord of Glamorgan, had bestowed on Margam Abbey the advowson of Aberavon Church, in his lordship, without the royal licence, asserting that he was one of the barons of the marches of Wales, that is a lord marcher, possessing within his lordship royal jurisdiction, and could therefore make the gift (which, however, he could not) without royal licence. Subsequently the abbey obtained papal permission to appropriate; but the crown, by a suit in the court of common pleas, recovered the advowson under the provisions of the statute of mortmain. Yet the king graciously gave licence for its appropriation for the sake of himself and his heirs, his and their souls, etc. Birch's *Margam*.

CHAPTER VI

John de Mowbray left, by Eleanor, daughter of William, lord Bourchier, sister to the earl of Essex, John de Mowbray his son and heir. He had already been created earl of Warren and Surrey by Henry VI., and succeeded, on his father's death, to the titles of duke of Norfolk, earl Marshal and Nottingham, and lord Segrave and Breos of Gower.

Upon the death in 1461 of the duke of Norfolk, the young duke's father, John Harper was (*Pat. Roll,* 1 Edw. IV., 1461) appointed, 'during good behaviour,' to audit the accounts of all bailiffs, etc,. of 'the king's lordships and castles of Gower, Kylvey, Bromfield, etc., late of the duke of Norfolk, deceased, and in the king's hands by reason of the minority of John, his heir.' And later in the year we find the appointment by patent, during the same minority, of William Herbert, lord Herbert, king's knight, to the custody of the lordships of Swaynesey, Gower, and Kelbey, in South Wales, and all castles, manors, etc., parcel of the same, with all royal rights , escheats, franchises, liberties, etc., rendering to the king 200 marks yearly.

In 1468 this William Herbert, lord Herbert, was created earl of Pembroke for his services to the king, particularly in the taking of Harlech Castle after it had long been gallantly held by a brave Lancastrian

A copy of a manuscript which has recently come into our hands, entitled, 'The True Succession of the lordship of Gower from the 1st Henry I. to 1623,' referring to the young duke of Norfolk, states that 'This John did in April, anno. 17 of Edw'd 4th, make away the seignory of Gower to the lord Will Herbert, earle of Pembroke, in exchange for other lands in England.' This would take us to the year 1478, nine years after the death of the earl of Pembroke at Banbury. Perhaps there is intended the 7th instead of the 17th year of Edward IV., when, in 1468, there certainly was an exchange of estates between the duke of Norfolk and the earl, the latter giving up lands in Norfolk and Suffolk which he had acquired, in place of Chepstow castle and manor and Todenham, and perhaps Gower.

But the succession and ownership of Gower at this period is surrounded with much mystery and confusion, for it appears to have been, at the same time, claimed as the possession of the earls of Pembroke (and later of the earl of Huntingdon), and also of the Norfolk family. Let us marshal the facts in chronological order.

We have spoken of the probable exchange of Gower with the earl of Pembroke, in 1468, and we assume the fact since subsequent evidence proves Gower to have been in the earl's possession, and it is not referred to in the inquisition post mortem of the duke of Norfolk in 1475. But we suspect that the lordship of Gower remained liable to certain charges upon it in favour of the duchess Eleanor, the young duke's mother. These charges appear to have been arranged on the 10th March, 5 Edw. IV., 1466. And we have a further suspicion that the duke of Norfolk did not give up possession of Gower to the first earl of Pembroke.

The earldom of Pembroke was conferred upon William Herbert, lord Herbert, according to Sir Harris Nicholas's descent of the earldom, on the 8th September, 1468, and the earl was beheaded on the following 27th July. He was succeeded by his son, another William, earl of Pembroke, who found himself immediately in a lawsuit with the duke of Norfolk over the ownership of the estates of Gower. Unfortunately we have no knowledge of the pleadings in the suit, but we know that the earl recovered Gower.

The evidence is found in the patent roll of 9 Edward IV.[1] The king confirmed, on the 3rd May, 1470, to William, earl of Pembroke (the second earl), the castle and manor of Swaneseye, the lordship or land of Gower, and the lordship or land of Kylvey, which he, the earl, had recovered in the Michaelmas term, 8th Edward IV. (1469), against John, duke of Norfolk, by a writ of the king of right *praecipe in capite,* directed to the sheriff of Hereford; and the entry states that the earl was then in seisin and possession of the same.

This brought out the claim upon the lordship of Gower by the duchess Eleanor of Norfolk, widow of John, duke of Norfolk, and mother of the then duke, who, according to the patent roll 9th Edward IV. (1470) (*Calendar,* p. 191), was described as 'late the wife of John, duke of Norfolk, tenant in chief.' She was granted an exemplification of 'an assignment made (on the 10th March, 5th Edward IV., 1466) in pursuance of John Harper, the younger, esquire, escheator, in the presence of John ap Griffith, attorney of the duke, viz., the castle, town, and lordship of Swaynesey, in the lordship of Gower, to the value of 11*l.* yearly; the castle manor and lordship of Pennarth, to the value of 18*l.* yearly; the manor and lordship of Lunon, to the value of 18*l.* yearly; the manor and lordship of Kythill, to the value of 4*l.* yearly; the englishery of Gower, alias the manor or lordship of Westgower, to the value of 9*l.* yearly; and 3 watermills and a fulling-mill in the parish of Swaynesey, to the value of 9*l.* yearly.

The date of this assignment, 1466, shews it to have been made by the duchess Eleanor's son, her husband having died five years earlier, and it is disappointing that there is no record available which informs us of the nature of this assignment, nor do we know if the lordship, when recovered by the earl of Pembroke, remained charged with the yearly indebtedness to the duchess.

At the death of the first earl of Pembroke, his son, William, who recovered Gower, was but a boy of nine years, and did not therefore attain his majority until 1481. During his minority, Gower would be in the king's hands, and the period of his minority was marked by the exchange, in 1480, of his title of earl of Pembroke for that of earl of Huntingdon (as to which more presently); but there arises the singular circumstance that in 1480 and 1481 the king made appointments of officers to the lordship of Gower, not as during the minority of the young earl of Huntingdon, as the earl then was, but (in 1480) 'during the minority of the king's kinswoman Anne, daughter and heir of John, late duke of Norfolk;' and (in 1481) during that of 'the king's second son, Richard, duke of York.'

Would it not appear that there was still some difficulty, not revealed in the records, surrounding the possession by the earl of Huntingdon of the lordship of Gower, and that the king still held it to be the property of the Norfolks, and their heiress?[2]

The entries we refer to are in the patent roll, 20th and 21st Edward IV., and are as follows:—

1480, 7th October. Grant to the king's servant, Thomas Vaughan, one of the esquires of the body, of the office of the custody of the Park of Prise, within the lordship and county of Gower in West Wales, and the office of coroner of the same lordship, during the minority of the king's kinswoman, Anne, daughter and heir of John, late duke of Norfolk. (Vaughan had, on the previous day, been granted a yearly rent of 20l. from the issues of the lordship of Gower, during the same minority.)

1481, 25th January. Appointment of the king's servant, John Thomas, one of the yeomen of the crown, to be receiver and approver of the lordship of Gower, during the minority of the king's kinswoman, Anne, etc.

1481, 10th November. Grant to the king's servant, Richard Hawte, the younger, esquire, of the office of steward of the lordship called Gowerslondez, and the office of constable of the castle of Swansey in Wales, during the minority of the king's second son, Richard, duke of York.

It is noteworthy that, in the deed of settlement (*Parliament Roll*, Vol, vi., p. 168) of the estates of Anne, duchess of Norfolk, in 1477, 'for the duke of York,' the king's second son, there is no mention of Gower.

Writing in the *Dictionary of National Biography* (Vol. xlviii., p. 185), Mr. James Gairdner tells us succinctly of the marriage of Anne de Mowbray, lady seignieur of Gower, with the king's second son, Richard, duke of York. The project was afoot before he was three and a half years old, and he was given the title of earl of Nottingham, held by the lately deceased duke of Norfolk, his intended wife's father. Seven months later he was made duke of Norfolk and earl Warren. The marriage was celebrated at St. Stephen's chapel, Westminster, on the 15th January, 1478, when both parties were in their sixth year.

'The object of the match,' says Mr. Gairdner, 'was avowedly to provide for a cadet of the royal family out of the funds of a wealthy nobleman whose line was now extinct, and parliament not only ratified an agreement with the duchess-dowager of Norfolk by which, in exchange for other lands, she gave up á large part of her jointure to the young couple, but enacted that the gift should remain the property of the duke of York, even if his wife died without issue.' (*Rolls of Parliament*, v. 168-170).

In a document, dated 5th May, 1479, appointing the duke of York lord lieutenant of Ireland, he is styled duke of York and Norfolk, and also earl of Surrey and Nottingham, earl marshal of England, and lord of Segrave, of Mowbray, and of Gower. Thus we find Anne, duchess of Norfolk, and her husband, to have been successively possessed of the lordship of Gower.

In 1481 the earl of Huntingdon came of age, and the king confirmed him in his possession of Gower, In 1482 an Act of Parliament effecting the settlement upon the duke of York, consequent on the death of Anne, his wife (*Parliamentary Rolls*, Vol. vi., p. 205), made the following provision in favour of the earl of Huntingdon, whose title was taken back to the lifetime of his father:—

Provided alway that this Acte ne eny thyng therin conteyned be not in any wise prejudiciall ne hurtfull to William Herbert, earl of Pembroke, nor to his heirs, by whatsoever name he was called, for the castles, lordships, and manors of Chepstowe, and Gower, with all their appurtenances in Wales and the marches of the same.

Provided also that this Acte extend not ne in no wise be prejudiciall unto John, Lord Howard, his heirs or his assigns, of or in any right, title, or interest, to him, his heirs or assigns belonging, in the lordship of Gower and Cheppestowe, with their appurtenances, this present Acte not withstanding.

It does not appear that there was any mature claim to Gower by John lord Howard,[3] who fell three years later (1485), whilst commanding the archers on the field of Bosworth. He did, however, succeed, jointly with the family of Berkeley to the inheritance of the house of Norfolk, through the marriage of Margaret and Isabel, the daughters of the first duke of Norfolk, so that he could, in certain events, have succeeded to the lordship of Gower.

Notwithstanding the earl of Huntingdon attained his majority in 1481, and that, according to the *Parliament Rolls*,[4] a patent of that year confirmed to him the castles, lordship, and manors of Chepstow and Gower, we find that two years later the king appointed a guardian or governor of Gower, so that the lordship was then in the hands of the crown.

The evidence of this is contained in a document preserved amongst the Harleian MSS. (No. 433), dated during the short three months of the reign of Edward V., in 1483. This was of the nature of letters of intendence to the officers, etc., of Gowerland, dated the 26th May, 1 Edward V., 1483, relating to the grant of the custody of Gower, dated the 16th of the same month. Herein the officers, farmers, and tenants of the lordship were ordered that 'incontinent upon ye sight hereof ye do avoide your selfe from ye possession and occupacion of any office belonging ye said Gowers lands,' and the document continues that by the advice of his 'derest oncle of Gloucester,[5] protector of this royme during our young age,' the king had committed the rule and governance of the lordship to Henry, duke of Buckingham,[6] to whom he had delegated the 'putting in and out of the officers there.'

It would appear that the earl of Huntingdon had fallen under the displeasure of the regent Buckingham, who saw an opportunity of possessing himself of the earl's estates. He therefore influenced the king to require the surrender of the lordship of Gower, justifying the action as being 'for the reformacon and the whole publique, restful governance, and ministration of justice, in South Wales, and for the satisfaction of grete and notable sommes of money diew[7] by the said earl of Huntingdon to the king.'

Thus the lordship of Gower had become vested in the crown during the reigns of Edward V. and Richard III. It remained for Henry VII. to make restitution. On the 24th October, 1485, that king granted for life to Walter ap David ap John the office of coroner of Gowersland; and on the 2nd August, 1487, he granted a pardon of arrears of accounts, and release of all actions to William Herbert, knight, lord Herbert . . . . alias William earl of Huntingdon.'[8] This pardon, doubtless, carried with it the restoration to the earl of the lordship of Gower.

[1] *Calendar Pat. Rolls*, 9 Edw. IV., p. 191.

[2] Some light on this subject may be gleaned from the *Parliament Rolls*, 1 Henry VII., which contain a petition by the heirs of one Thomas Charles, a Norfolk landowner, which latter appears to have agreed to hand over to Lord Herbert lands which Herbert intended to exchange with John de Mowbray, duke of Norfolk, for Gowerslonde and Chepestowe. The petition states that the agreement had been extorted from Thomas by force, whilst he was imprisoned in the Tower by King Edward IV., on suspicion of treason. 'To hym came William, Lord Herbert, afterwards called earl of Pembroke, and put hym in feare of hys lyfe, without any comforts in that behalfe, unto the tyme the said Thomas for his deliverance out of the said prison would grant and agree to deporte from his aforesaid manors of Kettilborrow and Sizelands . . . . . The said Thomas Charles, only for fear of destruction, and in avoiding the jeopardy of his life, did conveye to the said duke of Norfolke all his above estates by the occasion of the imprisonment and menaces of my Lord Herbert.' The petition

prayed for the setting aside of the agreement made under duresse, saving a life interest in favour of Elizabeth, duchess of Norfolk. The petition was answered: 'Soit fait come il est desire.' It appears from the foregoing that the exchange was meditated at the coronation of Edward IV., when Lord Herbert was created Lord Herbert of Raglan, Chepstow, and Gower, the duke of Norfolk to have estates in Norfolk, in exchange for Chepstow and Gower, which were to go to the titular lord. (*Vide* also *Materials illus. of the reign of Henry VII.*, Vol. i., p. 126.)

[3] Later on, Thomas, the third Howard duke of Norfolk, was created earl of Surrey, earl marshal, and high treasurer of England, lord Mowbray, Seagrave, and Breos of Gower. His eldest son, Henry, was, in his father's lifetime, beheaded on Tower-hill, and his (Henry's) son, Thomas Howard, was 'restored in blood' by Queen Mary, and made 4th duke of Norfolk, etc., and lord Breos of Gower. For proposing a marriage with Mary Queen of Scots, however, he was attainted, beheaded on Tower-hill June, 1572, and buried in the Tower chapel.

[4] *Pat Rolls,* 22 Ed. IV., p. 207.

[5] By whom, it will be remembered, the boy king, Edward V., was, with his brother, who was lord of Gower, stated to have been smothered in the Tower. They were sons of Elizabeth Woodville (queen of Edw. IV.), to whose hand Sir Hugh Johnys, of Swansea, had previously aspired.

[6] Another victim of Gloucester's hatred, who, as Richard III., caused him to be beheaded.

[7] This was not the first time that the lordship of Gower had been taken by the crown for debt, for King John seized it from the first De Breos, lord of Gower, although animosity entered as much into that transaction as the circumstance of long credit.

[8] *Memorials illustrative of the reign of Henry VII.*, Vol. ii., p. 161. The earl is described as 'William Herbert, knt., Lord Herbert, *alias* late earl of Pembroke, late chamberlain in South Wales, *alias* late chamberlain of Edward, late prince of Wales, *alias* William Herbert, late earl of Pembroke, son, heir, and tenant of the lands of William, late earl of Pembroke, *alias* William, earl of Huntingdon.' Thus the pardon and release covered the liabilities of the present earl and his late father.

CHAPTER VII

END OF THE NORFOLK REGIME. ANNE DE MOWBRAY LORD OF GOWER
MARRIES PRINCE RICHARD, DUKE OF YORK. THE HERBERTS IN
POSSESSION. GWILYM DDU O RAGLAN LEADS HIS MEN OF GOWER AT
BANBURY. A DOCUMENTARY PICTURE OF SWANSEA IN 1478.

Having now completed our digression, undertaken in order to present
these difficulties in the succession of the lordship, we may return to our
main narrative. We have already, however, told at sufficient length the
story of the marriage arranged, and at an early year solemnized, between
Anne, the only daughter of the last of the Mowbrays, dukes of Norfolk and
lords of Gower, with the youthful duke of York, the second son of Edward
IV. Surviving her father, the child Anne became duchess of Norfolk and
lady seignieur of Gower; and her husband surviving her also became lord
of Gower, the claims of the earl of Pembroke and his son, afterwards earl
of Huntingdon, being apparently in abeyance.

But some particulars must be given of so famous a personage as the earl
of Pembroke, who had designed to possess the lordship of Gower. This was
William Herbert ('Gwilym ddu o Raglan'), son of Sir William ap Thomas
('Y marchog glas o Went'), who was born in 1423, knighted for his exploits
in France, and was the great Welsh personality in the Wars of the Roses,
and who shared in the distribution of the confiscated estates and offices of
the earl of Warwick in 1460. But later in that year he joined the Yorkist
Warwick, and became one of the small number, of whom John, duke of
Norfolk and lord of Gower, was another, who were responsible for
proclaiming, 4th March, 1461, the earl of March as King Edward IV., an
incident which has been described as 'a Welsh triumph, and the very soul
of it Sir William Herbert.'[1] 'His reward,' says Mr. H. T. Evans, 'was
immediate and great, and amongst the honours given him at the
coronation was the title of Lord Herbert of Raglan, Chepstow, and
Gower.' The title did not carry with it ownership of Gower, for the
lordship still remained in heirship to young De Mowbray.

Swansea Castle was not in a condition to play any part in the Wars of the
Roses, being, as we have seen, only a ruin; but Oystermouth Castle had
been strengthened and victualled, and was put in charge of Sir Hugh
Johnys, of Swansea, as constable[2] in 1461 (April 1st, and confirmed 25th
November), for which position he was granted 20 marks a year.

Soon after gaining his title, Lord Herbert was, in 1461, deputed to clear
out the Lancastrians from South Wales, and this he quickly effected, and
received further rewards; he was made sheriff of Glamorganshire for life,
and chief justice and chamberlain of South Wales; and was given many

other offices of importance in the counties of Carmarthen, Cardigan, Brecon, and Monmouth, and North Wales. From this time forward he devoted himself to close personal attendance on the king, and when, in 1464, a fierce engagement broke out at 'Drusslyn,' in Carmarthenshire, between the Lancastrians, Hopkin ap Rhys, of Llangyfelach, Philip Mansel,[3] of Swansea, and Oxwich, and Lewis ap Rhydderch ap Rhys, of Strata Florida, a monk, on the one side, and the Yorkists, the Dwnns of Kidwelly,[4] on the other, it was our John lord Mowbray, lord of Gower,[5] who was despatched to quell it and the rioting in Wales which supervened.

Lord Herbert's intimacy with the king led to the open jealousy of Warwick, which that doughty warrior sated by bringing Herbert to the headsman's block. The fall of Harlech Castle,[6] the last stronghold of the Lancastrians, owing to Herbert's military prowess, was followed by the grant to Herbert of the earldom of Pembroke (as we have stated) in 1468, in which year he 'recovered' the lordship of Gower from the duke of Norfolk. In 1469 he hastily brought together 10,000 Welshmen for the historic engagement at Banbury that was to terminate for him with his life.

During this recruiting the earl arrived at Llandilo-vawr, where (on the 16th July),[7] he made his will at the altar in the church, reserving 4000 marks of his own money in his pocket to defray his costs. On the field of Banbury he was taken prisoner, as well as his brother, Sir Richard Herbert, of Coldbrook, and by his enemy, Warwick, ordered to be beheaded, a sentence which was carried out two days later.[8]

It is worthy of being recorded how splendidly the men of Wales were represented in these sanguinary engagements. The earl of Pembroke's Welsh contingent of 6,000 and over (some say 13,000), to which Gower largely contributed, was claimed to be 'the best in Wales.' At Edgecote (Banbury), on the 26th July, the Welshmen were attacked with a shower of arrows, in which arms the men of Gower and Gwent had, as in earlier times, shewn conspicuous proficiency; but now there was a shortage of arrows, and the bowmen were compelled to descend from their stronghold to the plain, where a fierce conflict was waged for several hours.

In this conflict Pembroke and his brother, Sir Richard Herbert, both behaved most valiantly. The latter, the doughty knight of Ewias, 'with his poleaxe in his hand, passed twice by force through the battle of his adversaries, and returned without mortal wound.' At the critical point of the engagement Warwick's men were reinforced by a large company of rabble and traitors, so that the Welshmen were broken and fled, about 5,000 being left dead on the field. Many prominent Welshmen were taken, besides Pembroke and his brother, including Thomas Vaughan and John Dwnn, of Kidwelly, who were removed to Banbury. Amongst those who were killed, according to William of Worcester, was Rice ap Morgan, of

Ilston, in Gower.[9]

The inquisition post mortem of the earl of Pembroke was taken the 22nd January, 9 Edw. IV. (1469-70), and he was shewn to have held 'in his demesne as of fee the castle and manor of Swanesey, the lordship or land of Gower, the lordship or land of Kylvey, the castle and manor of Oystermouthe, the castle and manor of Lloughor, and the manors of Landymore, Russely, Kythull, Trewydva, Lunon, Pennard, and West Gower, with their appurtenances,' the said castles, etc., being held of the king as of the crown, and were worth by the year £120 10s. 4d.'

The earl of Pembroke's death brought the succession of the lordship of Gower to his son, William, now earl of Pembroke. He surrendered the earldom to King Edward IV., who delivered it to his son, Prince Edward; and Herbert was thereupon (4th July, 1479) created earl of Huntingdon. He was but nine years old at his father's death, according to the inquisition of the latter, and would reach his majority 5th March, 1481.

One of the Ministers' accounts of this period is preserved in the muniment-room at Badminton, and it is printed here because of its intrinsic and topographical interest. It is for the year 1478-9,[10] and is as follows:—

The account of John Cradock,[11] portreeve there during the time aforesaid (1478-1479):

Arrears.—The same renders account of £17 12s. for the arrears of the last account of the year next preceding, as appears there at the foot. Sum £17 12. 0d.

Rents of Assize with increase rent.—And for £9 0s. 15d. for rents of Assize there yearly payable at the terms of Easter and St. Michael equally; and for 6s. 8d. for the farm of the wear there, which late was of Thomas Charles, payable yearly at the Feast of St. Michael only, and for 12s. for the rent of the wears there yearly, viz., one of Thomas Dawkyn (6d.), one in the tenure of Richard Key (6d.), one in the tenure of the said Richard (6d.), one in the tenure of Thomas Dawkyn (6d.), one in the tenure of John Key (6d.), one in the tenure of William Sewyn (6d.), one called Dribed (6d.), one called Fullerswere (6d.), one in the tenure of Walter William (12d.), one in the tenure of David Malefaunt (12d.), one in the tenure of Richard Tomlyn (12d.), one called Abbottswere (12d.), one in the tenure of John ap Gr (12d.), and one in the tenure of John Davy (12d.), and for 12d. for one wear in the tenure of John Powcock, let to him at farm this year.[12]

And for 2d. for the farm of the Pole and the Ford [13] there this year, let to farm to John ap Jevan Melyn, Rees ap G'llm, and William ap Jevan ap Henry; for 6d. late coming from one gravelly place[14] near the sea there, nothing this year because no profit did therefrom come nor could be received. But he answers for 6s. 8d. for one piece (of land) of Thomas Chambers of the grant of John, late duke of Norfolk, and for 6d. for increase rent of one curtilage, late of Nicholas Clerke, yearly at the terms aforesaid, and for 12d. for the rent of one acre of land in the Bouteyn,[15] this year at the same terms.

For 13s. 4d. for the farm of the orchard.[16] that William ap Thomas Dawkin claims to have for the term of his life of the grant of John, late duke of Norfolk and lord of Gower and Kilvey, by letters patent of the said late duke thereof, made to the same William. Nor for 26s. 8d. for the farm of the passage there, formerly 40s., nothing charged this year because the said parcel is charged together in the title of farms. But he answers for 2s. 6d., for the rent of half a burgage, late of Felix Baker, demised this year, besides 6d. yearly for the ancient free rent thereof. For 6s. 8d. for the farm of Portmeade, nothing here because hereinafter in the title of farms.

But he answers for 3s. for a little garden lately made in the Boylathe[17] there this year, at the terms aforesaid, and for 12d. for the rent of one new garden in the Westrete,[18] within the town of Swaynsey, this year, so lately demised to William Harold yearly, And for 6d. for the new rent of one parcel of land, upon which is erected one mill, for sharpening knives, axes, and other iron instruments, [20] so demised to John Gr, this year. And for 15s. 4d. for new rent of John Weston, lately accruing to the lord in default of heirs so demised this year. And for £6 7s. 11d. for increase rent of divers lands and tenements within the town of Swensey and in the Fields[21] of the said town, as appears in the account of the Reeve there of the 17th year of the reign of King Henry the 6th, whereof Thomas, late duke of Norfolk and lord of Gower and Kilvey, at the time and in the 21st year of the reign of Richard the second, was seized by the hands of the Reeve of the aforesaid town of Swaynsey, as in the account of the said year more fully appears.

For one penny for one parcel of land near the ditch,[22] or for 12d. for the rent of the Smelting house[23] near the Castle there, formerly of Henry Conneway, which was wont to render yearly 4s. 8d., or for one piece, late of Thomas Gr., which was wont to render yearly 3d., or for 6s. 8d.,[24] late coming for the rent of one burgage, late in the tenure of John Davy, or for three wears in the waters of Tawe, or for 6s. 8d., late for the farm of one mill, newly built between the water and the toure, late in the tenure of Ievan ap Eynon, nothing this year nor for many years past for want of a tenant and repairs, as is testified upon the account. Sum £17 18s. 7d.

Divers Farms.—And for £11 for the farm of three water and corn mills and one fulling mill there, demised to Gro ap Ievan Voia, William ap Henry, Jevan Gwyn, and John Tomkin for the term of 16 years, by indenture, dated the 4th day of April in the said 16th year, the mills aforesaid to be repaired at their proper costs in all things, except great timber, iron, and stones, and at the end of the said term deliver up the said mills sufficiently repaired, and provided that they be competently repaired at the beginning of the said term, at the cost of the lord, etc. And for 13s. 4d. for the farm of the orchard, so demised this year. And for 12s. for the farm of one parcel of land, called Ilond and Redmedowe, so demised this year. And for 40s. for the farm of the Boat and Passage there, so demised to Hopkin Weith this year. And for 6s. 8d. for the farm of the Meadow, called Portmede, so demised this year, and for 4d. for the farm of the wear there, demised to Ievan ap Ll'n this year, and for 3d. for the rent of one garden, late in the tenure of Nicholas William, demised to Margaret Mouce this year, but was wont to render 6d. yearly. And for 3s. 9d. for the rent of divers parcels of land there acquired and found by examination upon the account. Sum, £14 16s.10d.

Toll of the Market with the Prisage of Ale.—And for 40s. for the farm of the Toll of the Pix, with the rent of Censars and . . . . . there so demised this year. And for £10 for the farm of the prisage of Ale there, so demised to Gr ap Ievan Voir this year, etc. Sum, £12.

Perquisites of Hundreds. For any profit coming for perquisites of hundreds there he answers not here because in the charges of the Cachepole there, as is contained in the account of this year, etc. Sum, nothing.

Sum total of the receipts with arrears, £62 7s. 5d.

Allowances and Decay of Rent.—The same accounts in allowances of the rent of Sleges[25] parke (6d.), one tenement, late of John Taillour (3d.), one of Rek Plas (6d.), of one garden (3d.) under the Castle called Cuttis Garden, one parcel (12d.) of land where there is one kiln for burning lime, one place called Newerke[26] (2s. 6d.) under the castle, one tenement of Thomas Chambour (12d.), one tenement called Addelers[27] (9d.) destroyed by the sand of the sea,[28] and one parcel of land near the county-house (6d.), called the Shirehall,[29] in the hands of the lord, whereof nothing is approved on the oath of the accountant and witnesses upon the account, 7s. 3d. And in allowances of the rent and farm of one tenement, held by Thomas Chambour, above charged at 6s. 8d., besides 12s. for chief rent of the same, whereof nothing is levied this year as is testified upon the account, and so in allowance of rent, 6s. 8d. And no allowance of the rent of one wear, called Charles Were, above charged at 6s. 8d., now in the hands of the lord, totally destroyed, whereof the issues is none, and so in decay of the rent this year, 6s. 8d. Sum, 20s. 7d.

Sum of the allowances, 20s. 7d., and he owes £61 6s. 10d., of which there is allowed to him 15s. 4d. for the rent of the land of John Weston, not levied as in preceding years because he is ignorant where that land lies, as is testified upon the account. And to him 6d. for the rent of the Smith's mill, because it is totally decayed, etc., and to him 13s. 4d., paid to John Tomkin, deputy of John Vauchan, receiver there, for the arrears of David Foureboure, reeve there, in the second year, preceding by the acknowledgement of the same John upon this account.

And to him 16d. paid to the said receiver for the arrears of Hopkin Weith, farmer of the passage there in the year next preceding, by the acknowledgement aforesaid. And to him 62s. 11d., paid to the same receiver for the arrears of John Thomas, portreeve there in the year next preceding, by the same acknowledgement. And to him 16s. 8d., paid to the same receiver for the farm of the passage there this year, by the acknowledgement aforesaid. And to him £4 3s. 11d., paid to the same receiver by the hands of the portreeve there this year, by the acknowledgement aforesaid. And to him £4 0s. 22d., paid the same receiver, by the hands of the farmer of prisage of Ale this year, by the acknowledgement aforesaid. And he owes £38 9s. 7½d. Of which there is Respital to him £12 15s. 10d. above charged among the arrears, and £6 7s. 11d. above in the title of rents of Assise, in one sum by itself, for increase rent of divers lands and tenements within the town of Sweynsey and in the fields of the same town, as appears in the account of the portreeve there for the 17th year of King Henry the 6th, there respited for the two years preceding, and this year, as in many years preceding, because he is ignorant where those lands and tenements lie, whereof the said increase ought to be levied. And he owes beyond £19 15s. 10½d., whereof

Super— Owen ap Griffith, for his rent at 5s. yearly above charged within
the rent of assize, viz., for the two years preceding and this year
behind 15s. 0d

David Foubore, portreeve there in the 16th year of
the now king . . . . 8s. 7d.

Hopkin Weithe, farmer of the passage there this year . . . . 23s. 4d.

Gruff ap Ievan Voia and others, farmers of the mills and
prisage of Ale there this year . . . . 38s. 7½d.

The same Gr. and others, farmers of the prisage of Ale this year . 118s. 2d.

John Cradock, portreeve there this year . . . . £9 2s. 2d.

As we have already remarked, the contents of the foregoing document are so full of information regarding the topography and circumstances of our town at this period as to warrant its being included here in full; it certainly gives us a particularly vivid picture of the Swansea of the late fifteenth century.

NOTES TO CHAPTER VII

[1] Howell T. Evans. William Herbert, earl of Pembroke, in *Trans. Cymm.*, 1909-10.

[2] *Cal. Patent Rolls* (1461-67), p. 81.

[3] Philip Mansel and Hopkin ap Rhys were amongst the leaders of the Welsh Lancastrian forces at Mortimer's Cross (2nd Feb., 1461), and they were reported to have been beheaded or captured there. William of Worcester (*Itinerarium*, p. 327) gives amongst the list of captured—'Philip Mansel, armiger, v mark annui valoris de Gowerland decapitatus; Hopkyn ap Rhys de Gowerland comitatu de Carmarthen decapitatus.' So far from this being the fact, however, both were in the field again in this later trouble in Wales, in 1464. Philip Maunsell, of Oxwich, appears amongst the many attainted persons named in the general act of this year (29th April, 1464), and a grant by the king, in the following year, vested his estates in Sir Roger Vaughan, the well-known Yorkist of Breconshire and Herefordshire, as also were those of Hopkyn ap Rees ap Hopkyn, with all issues from both estates from the 4th March, 1 Edward IV. (*Calendar of Patent Rolls*, 1465, p. 427). Philip Mansell is here not referred to as being deceased, and so a suggestion, which has been made, that he was captured by Sir Roger Vaughan, at Druslyn, and afterwards beheaded, is not tenable. Indeed, he was alive in 1485, for in the Parliament of 7th Nov. (1 Henry VII.) the attainders of 'Philip Maunsell, late of Oxenwike in Gowers land in South Wales, and Hopkyn ap Rys, late of Laganalough (Llangavelach) in Gower' were reversed, 'and their possessions restored to them.' (*Materials illus. of the reign of Henry VII.*, Vol. i., p. 116.) We appear to have no record of the exact date of Philip Mansell's death. His daughter, Jane, m. Sir Mathew Cradock, of Swansea; and his son, Jenkin, was father of Sir Rice Mansell, who bought Margam from King Henry VIII.

[4] Sir John Dwnn was amongst the prisoners of Banbury who were beheaded.

[5] Mr. H. T. Evans, in his article on 'William Herbert, earl of Pembroke' (*Trans. Cymm.*, 1909-10), is at a loss to account for this circumstance, and suggests that the task should have been given to William, Lord Herbert, but that he was at this time in attendance at court, as the king's most confidential friend. Mr. Evans had, apparently, not observed that the duke of Norfolk was lord of Gower.

[6] For this accomplishment Herbert's brother, Sir Richard Herbert of Ewias, appears to have been jointly responsible.

[7] Dudgale's *Baronage*, Vol. ii., p. 257.

[8] It is recorded how 'entreaty was made for Sir Richard, both for his goodly person, which excelled all men there, and also his chivalry on the field of battle.' The earl of Pembroke, when he should lay his head down on the block, said: 'Let me die, for I am old, but save my brother, who is young, lusty, and hardy, mete and apt to serve the greatest prince in Christendom.' G. T. Clark says that the earl was beheaded upon the cill of the church porch at Banbury.

[9] H. T. Evans: *Wales and the Wars of the Roses*, pp. 182-2.

[10] The account is for the year in which the Lord Herbert of Gower surrendered to the king the title of earl of Pembroke, and received that of earl of Huntingdon; but the account bears no reference to this circumstance.

[11] John Cradock was doubtless of the notable family of Cradock of Gower already referred to, of whom Sir Mathew Cradock, in the next generation, was the central figure.

[12] The Inquisition post mortem of John de Mowbray, taken 1432-3, accounts for only 'three wears in the water of Tawye, of the annual value of 5s. 4d;' and that of Earl Thomas de

73

Beauchamp, of 1369, refers to 'divers wears in the water of Tawy,' let at farm for 100s. per ann. In this Ministers' Account, one wear is let at 6s. 8d., 14 let at 12s., and one at 12d. It is evident that wears were erected and removed at the convenience of farmers, and we are given the impression that fishing in the Tawe in these days must have been a profitable pursuit.

[13] There were anciently two fords at Swansea; one where the river fell into what was later known as Fabian's Bay, some little distance below the ferry; and another at the other extremity of the town, opposite what became Morris's-lane of the eighteenth century. That here referred to was the former, and near it was the 'Pole of Perch,' and we have explained how it may have been at the pole that river tolls were levied in our *History of the Port of Swansea*, p. 26.

[14] Evidently a gravel pit which had been worked out.

[15] We suspect the 'Bouteyn' to have been an early use of the word 'Bovetown,' which was formerly the designation of High-street.

[16] The orchard, which gave its name to Orchard-street, will be referred to later.

[17] 'Boylathe.' It would appear as if the scribe had attempted to write 'Borlache,' as at this time Burlake, and later Burlais, was spelt; the written *ch* is often difficult to distinguish from *th*, and it is possible that a long *r* could be read as *y*.

[18] Westrete is one of the puzzles of Swansea nomenclature. College-street seems to be its present equivalent.

[19] Harold and Weston as Swansea surnames were of antiquity even at this time.

[20] Further on this is called 'Smiths mill, totally destroyed.'

[21] The fields of the town, that portion of the whole borough, distinct from the town, and called the Franchise until quite modern times.

[22] The ditch, supplied by the rivulet falling down the Mount Pleasant of later days, formed the ditch or moat around the town walls.

[23] A smelting house near the castle at this time was an early instance, and it had evidently been established for a considerable period. Col Francis, in his *Copper Smelting*, states that traces of the furnaces had been found in the 19th century.

[24] The sum of 6s. 8d. (half a mark) can hardly have been a true burgage rent. Probably this represents a part of the lord's demesne let out to a tenant at will.

[25] Sleges is one of many place-names in this document, which can scarcely now be recognised; but 'park' was a field or close.

[26] This may possibly be explained as some new work carried out under the castle.

[27] Mr. C. A. Seyler obliges us with the following suggestion regarding 'Addelers' as a local place name:—'I suspect this may contain the root of the Welsh *arddel*, as in arthel-man—advocarius. *Arddel* appears in Anglicised form as arthel. Addelers was possibly of the arthel-men, or advocarri in the lord's protection. The Welsh word for advocating is *arddlwr*, which corresponds very well with Addeler.'

[28] The sea has ever encroached into Swansea Bay, but the sand-drift has not been so continuous. Probably this particular destruction of land by the sand took place at the time of the besanding of Pennard and Penmaen on the south coast of Gower.

[29] 'the County-house, called the Shirehall,' was the hall provided after the destruction of the castle, for the holding of the courts of those parts of the lordship of Gower (outside Swansea, which was the chief town), which had no manor courts of their own. There was, as distinct from the county-house, a town-house wherein the corporate administration of Swansea was transacted.

CHAPTER VIII

SUCCESSION OF THE HOUSE OF WORCESTER AND BEAUFORT. END OF
THE LORDSHIP MARCHER OF GOWER. GOWER ABSORBED INTO
GLAMORGAN. LAWSUIT RELATIVE TO INCLOSURES AND
ENCROACHMENTS. PRIVILEGES GRANTED TO THE LORD OF GOWER.
OLIVER CROMWELL, LORD OF GOWER.

The career of William Herbert, earl of Huntingdon and lord of Gower, was not an eventful one. He married Mary, fifth sister and co-heiress of Richard Woodville, Earl Rivers, and had one child, Elizabeth, who married Charles Somerset, first earl of Worcester (base son of Henry Beaufort, duke of Somerset), who, therefore, became Lord Herbert of Gower in his wife's right.

Charles Somerset was, as Dugdale[1] tells us, 'a person of great parts,' and of 'very high advancements in those times wherein he lived,[2] as well in honour as estate.' Amongst the honours to which he attained was that of admiral of the king's fleet at sea, 3 Henry VII. (1485). Dugdale asserts that these 'eminent favours' were 'the chief furtherances to his marriage with Elizabeth, the sole daughter and heir to William Herbert of Huntingdon.' On the 26th Nov., 1506, he was, by patent, created Baron Herbert of Raglan, Chepstow, and Gower in his own right. He received a grant, 1st Henry VIII (1509), of the governorship, and the next year the constableship, of the castles of Cardiff, Cowbridge, and Neath. Henry was particularly partial to his kinsman (both being descended from Owen Tudor), and constituted him lord chamberlain for life, and, in 1514 (1st February, 5 Hen. VIII), advanced him to the dignity of earl of Worcester. He died in 1526, and was buried in St. George's chapel, Windsor.

To him succeeded, as second earl of Worcester, Henry Somerset, his only son by his first wife, Margaret, daughter of William Courtenay, earl of Devon, and Katherine, his wife, daughter of Edward IV.[3] It may be recorded that earl Charles married secondly Elizabeth, daughter of Sir Anthony Browne, and by her had eight children, of whom Jane married Sir Edward Mansell, of Margam, knight.

There is in the muniment-room at Badminton a record of much interest, a vellum-covered book endorsed:—'Survey, &c., of Gower, &c., and other Estates in South Wales, in the reigns of Henry VIII, Queen Mary and Queen Eliz.' The following extract therefrom is of considerable value:—

Here ensueth the lands recou'ed (recovered) by my lorde Cardynalle grace and others, whereof they be seysed by force of the same recou'ye, and of the w'ch the use of the fee sympell ys dyscended to Henry nowe Erle of Worcester by ryghtfull cours of enherytance after the death of Elyzebeth daughter and heyre of Will'm late erle of huntingdo' moder of the seyd Henrye and late wyfe of Charles late erle of Worcester who had the sayd lands yn use durynge hys lyfe and the valour (value) of the same lands:

ffyrst the Castell and towne of Swanseye the lordshipp or man's of Gower and Kylveye, the Castell and manor of lloghor, the Castell and manor of Oystermouthe, and the mann's of Pennarthe and llonnon yn Southwales holden of the Kynge in capite, w'ch be worthe by yere cc li.

It is worthy of note that Charles Somerset, earl of Worcester, enjoyed the use of the fee simple of Gower during his life, but that it had legally passed to his son Henry on the death of his mother. In the same manner, the death of the lady Elizabeth[4] deprived earl Charles of his seat in the house of peers in respect of the title of 'lord Herbert and of Gower' which he had held in her right; and it was in consequence thereof that he was, as already stated, created in his own right baron Herbert of Raglan, Chepstowe, and Gower, in 1506.

With regard to the statement in the foregoing extract that Gower was amongst lands which had been recovered by cardinal Beaufort, the circumstances of the recovery are unknown to us, and we have sought unsuccessfully for some enlightenment on the subject. Marsh, the careful and resourceful annalist of Chepstow, does not mention the fact, although Chepstow would have been included in the recovery. It will be remembered, of course, that Charles Somerset was an illegitimate member of the house of Beaufort, earls of Somerset.

Not long after his succession, earl Henry granted, on the 8th October, 1526, a lease to 'Syr Mathias Cradok, knight,' of Swansea, of all the 'Mynes of Coles now founde or that hereafter can be founde, and also all the coles of the same mynes, w'in the said lordships of Gower and kylvey or the membres of the same,' from the previous Michaelmas for eighty years, for a payment of eleven pounds yearly. With the knowledge which we have today of the coal resources in the lordship of Gower, the leasing of all the coal for a yearly payment of eleven pounds is a thing to smile at.

Two matters of considerable importance to Swansea and Gower arose during the lifetime of earl Henry, viz., the granting of a charter affecting Swansea, and the abolition by Henry VIII. of the lordships marchers and the final extinction of their powers.

As to the charter granted in 1532, in which Swansea shares the privileges which it conveys, it is singular that it finds no place in Col. George Grant Francis's *Charters of Swansea*; the more so because this painstaking antiquary was in correspondence with the duke of Beaufort's steward and solicitor of his Gower estates, in 1871, and endeavoured to secure a complete list of the Swansea charters. As this charter of 1532 was not mentioned, it is probable there is no copy of it preserved in the muniment-room at Badminton.

The charter is dated the 18th September, 1532, and is of the nature of an agreement or deed of composition between the earl of Worcester and representatives of the several classes of tenants (freeholders of the englishery, tenants of the welshery, and tenants of Kilvey). Its opening clause runs as follows:—

Henry, earl of Worcester, of the one party; Leyson, abbot of Neth,[5] Syr Rice Mawnsell, Knight, George Herbert, Squier, Thomas Johns, Squier, Jamys Thomas, Harry Barett, John Franklen, John Cradock, John Synt John, William ap Rees Llwyd, Hopkyn Dawkyn, John D'd Morgan, Jankyn Francklen, David Mauncell', John Parkyn, John Grenow, Thomas ap Owein and Richard Thomas of the englishery of Gower, freeholders; And also Gw'lym Jankyn, Henry ap Jankyn, Hopkyn ap John, Richard ap John, D'd ap Rice ap John, Wyll'm Gryffyth, Dauid ap Gruffyth, and Rogger ap Owein, tenauntis, of the Welschere of Gower; And allso Thomas ap Meyrike ychen, John D'd ap Hopkyn, John ap D'd, Jankyn ap John, Dauid ap Hopkyn, and John Thomas vechan' of Kylvey on the other party.

The terms of the charter (which is printed at length in Birch's *History of Neath Abbey*, 1902, pp. 254-260) are such that, in consideration of the sum of 300 marks granted to the use of the earl, he agrees that De Breos's charter of 1306 to the tenants of Gower should be confirmed to the tenants of the 'lordschepp of Gower and Kylvey,' and further provisions are made for the regulation of the inhabitants of Swansey. De Breos's charter was to remain in force in all details 'exceptyng alwais the bonde of the thousant powndes contaigned and specified in the same chartour which shall remayn and be of such strength and force as it ws before the makyng heroff and non otherwise.'

The document is of considerable length, and deals with concessions and privileges given to the tenants of Gower, but for the purpose of our History the clauses relating to Swansea itself are alone reproduced.

Item where of olde tyme it was derectit be burgesses of the town of Swansey if eny tennantes of the seid lorscheppe or any other foren persens made eny frey and drue blod apon eny other man be violens apon the sonday in the seid towne that he or thei that so offende to the disterbaunce of the burgesses and inhabitauntes of the seid towne schalbe mercyd in xls. and jd. whiche mercement is nowe advertit and retorne apon the burgesses of the town of Swansey contrary to thentent of the seid ordenaunce and decre and allso contrary to the chartour of the towne. The seid Erle mendyng the quietnes and welth of his seid pure burgesses willith grauntith and covenanth that from hencefordd ther schall be no suche pynalltey or mersement levide ne gederd apon eny of the seid burgessis so that the same burgesses and inhabitauntes do endeuer them sylfe to do suche transgressours and offenders to be arestid and put under swertys for the seid mersement of xls. jd. but that the seid mercement only levyde and had of foren persons or person as sch(a)ll comytte suche offences and mysdemenours within the seid towne apon ther swrtes acordyng to thententh and meenige of the seid ordinances and (more) ouer that the seid Erle promissyth grauntith and covenantith to afirme allwey suche ordinaunce as schall be devisyd anu made be portre' and burgeses of the seid town not beying nor sownyng (sseeming) to the derogacion or prejudice of the seid Erle or his heirys and that as (for) such penallty as schall be cessed and ratyd be portrey for tyme beyng for brekyn of eny party of the seid ordenaunce the one halfe

77

theroff shcalbe leveyd to thuse of the seid Erle[6] and the tother halfe to the commyn cofyr of the seid towne for the commyn welthe of the seid town Also the seid Erle grauntith for hym and is heiris that from hensforth the stewarde of the seid lordscheppe of Gower' for the tyme beyng upon compaynt to hym made be prtre and burgesses of the seid town of Swansey schall have auctorite and power to exclude and exile all maner artificeres and hondycryfte men wiche from hensforth vse mistery of cuttynge and kervyng owte of the seid towne within the circuyte of vij miles of the seid town onles such artificeres be inhabitynge withyn the seid town of Swansey prouidyd all weisse that presente artificeres extend not to smythis nor tayloures al'so the portre' of the seid town for the tyme beyng schall electe and poynt too burgesses of the seid town to serche all suche tannyd lether as schall come to the seid town or schall be tannyd in the seid town so that the seid burgesses may se the seid tanerys haue no leder but that that schall be good abyll' and lawfull' apon the peyn of the forffeture of the same lether so insoficient and the tanner also to forfet for euery hyde so insufficiently tannyd vjs. viijd. the on halfe of the seid forfetures to the vse of the seid Erle and tother to thuse of the commyn cofer of the seid town of Swansey.

A general concession was added which affected the earl's tenants and the inhabitants of Swansea, and it provided that no tax ('taske') or tallage should be levied on them for five years from the date of the charter.

We shall see presently that, under the powers of this charter, there were annually appointed at the leet court of the manor of Swansea triers and searchers of leather, whose duties are explained by the charter, and were of much service to an important guild of traders in the town, of which, however, no records have been preserved.

The time had now arrived when the vain attempts of several monarchs to withdraw the powers so long exercised by the lords marchers of Wales were to be followed by the total extinction of those privilieges and concessions; and when also the union of Wales with England was to fully mature. In 1534 we find Henry, earl of Worcester, lord of Raglan, Chepstow, Gower and Kilvey, still issuing processes for the lordship of Gower 'in cancellaria nostra apud Sewensey,' and also causing parties to be summoned 'coram senescallo nostro comitatus nostri Gower seu ejus locumtenente ad comitatum nostrum apud Sewensey.' But the period of this local government was fast expiring.

Whatever opinion we may have formed of the character of Henry VIII., we must acknowledge that Wales is under a deep obligation to him for the statesmanlike measures of government which he passed. Edward I. had effectually stopped any extension during or after his time of the lordship marcher system of possessing territory by invading it. By his subjection of the last Llewelyn, prince of Wales, the king acquired for England the princely rights in Wales, and no further encroachments could be suffered on the part of his subjects. Later on the lord marchers' powers had been further curtailed by the establishment of the president and council of the marches, in the reign of Edward IV. But now, by Henry VIII., by virtue of the statute of his 27th year (1536), the lordship marchers were finally dissolved and divided into five counties, four of which, Radnor, Brecknock, Montgomery, and Denbigh, were declared to be in Wales, and Monmouth became an English county, the lords marchers, by this and subsequent statutes, being reduced to the position of English lords of manors. .

The Act of 27 Henry VIII. also constituted a new county by the consolidation of Gower and Kilvey with Glamorgan and Morganwg. The section dealing with this reform runs as follows:—

The lordshipes townes parishes hundredes and cantredes of Gower, Kelvey, Byshopstowne, Landaff, Signith supra, Signith subtus, Miskins, Ogmore, Glynothney, Tallagarne, Ruthein, Tallavan, Lamblethian, Lantwide, Theriall, Owan, Neth, Landewy, and the Clayes, and all honnours, etc., and heredities shalbe guildable and parcell of the Countie of Glamorgan. The shire of Glamorgan and Morgynocke and all the hundreds united unto it shalbe called by the name of the shire of Glamorgan only and by noe other.

Justice shal be administred to the subjectes and inhabitantes of the Countie of Glamorgan according to the lawes and customes and statutes of England as it is in the three sheires of Northwales and after noe Welsh lawe.

Thus the people of Gower and Kilvey, in common with all their neighbours in Wales, were placed on a footing of absolute equality with the people of England, and they have cause to remember with gratitude the privileges thus conferred upon them by bluff king Hal. In future, all original and judicial writs, indictments for treason, felony, and trespass, and all manner of process, should be made only in the king's name, and all offences committed against the peace should be considered as offences committed against the king and not against the peace of any other person. In this manner the excessive powers, such as *jura regalia* in lordships marchers passed away in favour of a more regular and uniform course of justice. Particularly the affairs of boroughs were now conducted by their own corporations instead of by the lord's stewards, and from this moment the records of the town of Swansea commence to be preserved for our use.

The first high sheriff of the newly-formed county of Glamorgan (for the 33 Henry VIII., 1541) was Sir George Herbert, knight, of Swansea, who was the second son of Sir Richard Herbert of Ewias, co. Monmouth, and grandson of Sir Mathew Cradock of Swansea; and who lived at the Place-house, which the last-named had built. Sir George Herbert was again high sheriff of the county for the 1st Mary, 1553; and he was steward in Gower for the earl of Worcester.

The introduction of the new regime appears to have been the signal for the committal of considerable depredations upon the territory of the earl by way of encroachments by the tenants of the lordship, which gave rise to a notable action in the Chancery of Queen Elizabeth. But of this we shall write presently.

At this time, too, be it noted, the act was passed for the dissolution of the chantries which effected the closing of the two centuries of beneficient work carried on in Swansea within the Hospital of the Blessed David of the foundation of the pious Henry de Gower, bishop of St. Davids.

Henry, the second earl of Worcester, lord of Chepstow and Gower, died on the 26th November, 1549, and was succeeded by his son William. But the latter did not apparently reach his majority for several years. In proof of this it may be stated that after the death of earl Henry, and on the 10th September, 1556, his widow, the Countess Elizabeth, with the consent of this son William, the heir apparent, granted to Sir George Herbert, knight, the Forest of Trewyddva, the following being the particulars extracted from the deed:—

Five parcels of waste land and pasture in the manor of Trewyddva in Gower Anglicana, whereof one parcel is called Forest Trewyddva, in length from the land of Hopkyn John David ap Hopkyn on the north part to the grain mill called Little Mill on the south, and in breadth having the river called Tawey on the east, and the highway (regalem viam) near the house of George ffrancklen towards Swansea on the west part.

Of the other four parcels, one is called Penyllan, another Dree Boeth, the third Gyn Gochu ('Goghe' = Goch in a confirmatory deed by earl William), and the fourth Pull y llyn, and all lying between the land of John ap Jevan Goghu on the east and that of Sir George Herbert otherwise Parke Jenkyn David Doon (Donne in the confirmation) on the west, the said parcel called Forest Trewyddva on the north, and the land of Sir George Herbert and the land of John Griffith ap Owen Gethin on the south. To hold the same of the countess and her heirs at the annual rent of 9s. 3d. in two equal portions, with suit of court of the manor and reliefs, and also rendering annually to the countess four pence for every wey of coal (carbonum) worked and taken from the said five parcels of land and sold.[7]

This grant was confirmed in the same year on the 20th December, by William himself, who had then succeeded to his inheritance.

Earl William, third earl of Worcester, and lord of Chepstow and Gower, caused a survey of his lordship of Gower to be made in 1583. It was taken by his son and successor, then Edward lord Herbert, by his brother-in-law Sir Edward Mansell, of Margam, and others, with a jury. The record thereof, so far as it appertains to Gower Anglicana, has been printed by the Cambrian Archaeological Association amongst a collection of *Gower Surveys*. This earl died on the 22nd February, 1587, and was followed by his son and heir Edward, fourth earl, and lord of Gower, &c., K.G. Queen Elizabeth made him master of the horse, largely because he was accounted to be the best horseman and tilter of the times.

This earl brought before the court of chancery, in the 36th Elizabeth (1595), a bill of complaint against Sir William Herbert, knight, Elizabeth Dawkin, widow, Philip John ap Rees, John William David ap Richard, Owen Penry, Lewis Griffith, Morgan John Morgan, William Thomas ap

Richard, John ap Owen, Thomas ap Jevan, Griffith ap Jevan, Hopkin John Griffith, Roger John ap Jevan, and others to the number of eighty, tenants of his seignories of Gower and Kilvey, and also a further complaint in general words against the whole of the tenants, numbering about a thousand persons.

He declared that his grandfather, Henry, earl of Worcester, was, about the 2nd Edward VI., seised in his demesne as of fee tail of the entire lordships manors and seignories of Gower and Kilvey, being of ancient time lordships marchers, with all their rights, royalties, &c., situate in the county of Glamorgan, within which lordships were other manors, &c., named in the plaint, together also with 'the manor or lordshipp marche of Kilvay aforesaid adionieng to the said seigniory of Gower,' whereof the earl was likewise seised in his demesne as of fee tail.

Within these lordships there were wastes, moors, customs, comorthes, pawnages, tolls, aids, mises, heriots, reliefs, perquisites, and other casualties appertaining to the lordships, time out of mind, and since the time named (2 Edward VI.) there had been 'wrongfully inclosed and encroached within the town and liberties of Swanzey divers parcells of the waste of the said town and manor of Swanzey, and then claimed as freehould' by the persons so encroaching.[8] Much abbreviated, the earl's complaints were as follows:—

Five acres in the southside, and adjoining to the hill there called Gibbett-hill, had been encroached by John David Vaughan; 200 acres adjoining to St. David's ditch, drawn in and encroached by Hopkin John Griffith; 30 acres, sometime parcel of a mead called Portmead, by John William David ap Richard, and Griffith ap Jevan; and 70 acres, divers parcels of the waste of Swanzey and of a meadow called Crowswood, alias Crowmead, drawn in and encroached, and then in the hands of Sir William Herbert, knight, his tenants and farmers.

In the manor of Trewyddva, another member of the seignory of Gower, the earl was seised of two parcels called Carne lloyd and Gwayny lleuereth, containing about 60 acres, in the occupation of the said Sir William Herbert, knight, one Roger John ap Jevan, George ffrancklyn, and divers others the tenants of the manor; and one wood or woody pasture called Coydtrewyddva, of 200 acres, in the occupation of the said Sir William Herbert, knight, John Landegg, George ffrancklyn, and other customary tenants.

Also in the manor of Gower Anglicana, another member of the seignory of Gower, the earl was seised of lands, arable and pasture, called Altbulden, Tir Du Ychan, and Tir Traherne grawgh, in the occupation of Elizabeth Dawkin, widdow, or her tenants, containing 50 acres; and in three parcels encroached by David Verley, parcel sometime of Gorsevawr and late in the occupation of the said Sir William Herbert, knight, of 26 acres; and of certain waste bounding west upon the pasture called the fforest of fairwood, since drawn in and divided in twelve parcels, containing about 220 acres, and then in the occupation of William John, John Thomas ap Henry, Sir William Herbert, knight, and others or their tenants; and of one parcel enclosed within ten years then last past, encroached from the waste called Pennard's moor, of 80 acres, by Elizabeth Dawkin, widow; and of one mead, commonly called the lords' mead, of which 5 parcels on the south side, containing about 50 acres, had been encroached by one William Dawkin and the said Elizabeth Dawkin; and a waste or pasture called Corse y cobb,

81

encroached by one John Price, gent, of about 20 acres.

Also the earl, at the time aforesaid, was seised of divers lands, meadows, arable, pasture, and woods, in the manors of Supraboscus and Subboscus, of about 300 acres, commonly called Keven y fforest, in the occupations of Robert John ap Owen, Morgan John Morgan, and Philip John ap Rees; and also of divers parcels of about 300 acres, commonly called Ridvugh or Rudvugh, in the occupations of John William David ap Richard, Morgan John Morgan, Griffith ap Jevan, Thomas Rees, and Rees ap Jenkin ap Jevan Donne, or their tenants; and in like sort the earl charged divers other tenants of the lordships or seigniories with such like enclosures and encroachments.

The earl claimed that the tenants of the manors of Supraboscus and Subboscus had always held of the manors by the true and ancient customs thereof, and there had always been the usage and custom that, at the death of every tenant without heir male, there was always due to the earl a rated and accustomed fine of 7s. for every acre so reverted for want of heir male, to be paid to the earl upon the admission of the next heir general, or the earl might grant the land to whom he pleased, all such grants being made by deed indented.

The tenants, however, so it was stated in the earl's plaint, claimed that they were seised in their demesnes as of fee of and in all their lands, etc., within the manors, although Henry, earl of Worcester, died seised of the premises, which descended to the late William, earl of Worcester, and after his death to the present earl, the plaintiff.

Furthermore, a thousand marks ought to have been paid to the new earl on his new entry into his estate for mises, and for aids to make his eldest son knight 100 marks, and for aids on the marriage of his eldest daughter 100 marks, all of which the tenants refused to pay or to confess to be due. The earl Edward, therefore, appealed to the court that all the encroachments, enclosures, mises, aids, comorths, gwobermerth, pawnage, serjeantie, tolls, etc., of which his grandfather and father had been seised might be restored to him. He prayed process of subpenas against all the whole tenants of the seignories. Whereupon divers tenants appeared and made their answers to the earl's plaint.

Mrs. Elizabeth Dawkin shewed that fifty years previously Hopkyn Dawkyn, deceased, was lawfully seised as of his demesne as of fee or fee tail, of divers tenements in the parishes of Swanzey and Ilston, Altbulden being one, and another being ffairwood and a parcel of waste of the west side of it called Bryn here, and always known as parcel of it. From Hopkyn Dawkyn it descended, about 40 years since, to William, as his son and heir, and again, 30 years since, on his death to his son and heir Jenkin Dawkin, and 13 years since, on his death, to his son and heir William Dawkin. He was the son of Jenkin and the defendant Elizabeth, and being a minor his mother and he entered into possession, and two years since William, seised of the estate, died, and it went to Elizabeth, Katherine, Alice, and Margaret Dawkin, daughters of Jenkin and Elizabeth, and, all being under age, the defendant and they entered into possession, as they were entitled to do so as they thought.

Sir William Herbert sought to establish his claim as being descended from Sir George

Herbert, knight, deceased, his grandfather, who long before the alleged encroachments was lawfully seised of the lands, and on his death, twenty years since, they came to the defendant as cousin and next heir of Sir George, being son and heir of Mathew Herbert, son and heir of the said Sir George, and he was prepared to establish his property in the same by divers ancient deeds and conveyances. He denied that he was guilty of any of the encroachments charged against him.

Other defendants having made similar claims to the lands, etc., which they were alleged to have encroached and enclosed, the plaintiff, the earl of Worcester, replied, and the defendants rejoined. Commissioners of the court of chancery examined the defendants and reported to the court, and a day of hearing was appointed (6th May, 1595).

As touching the plaintiff's claim for mises, it then appeared to the court, both by a patent under the hand and seal at arms of John, duke of Norfolk, then lord of the lordships or seignories, and by divers accounts proving payments of sums of money for mises by the tenants to Charles, sometime earl of Worcester, and also because mises were customarily paid in lordships marcher in Wales, that such mises were due to the said earl, but because there was no written evidence as to the amount of the mises, the court ordered, with the assent of the earl who was then in court, that a commission should enquire and determine what or how many mises ought to be made, and after what rate the tenants should contribute thereto, and the same commission was to make a similar enquiry and determination as to aids. The court also decreed that because the supposed encroachments and other matters in the plaintiff's bill were more appropriate to be decided by the common law, they should be dismissed out of the court for the purpose of such decision.

The foregoing document is particularly interesting as throwing light upon the statements in Cromwell's survey of Gower, to be referred to presently, that parts of 'Crow wood' had been enclosed by Sir William Herbert some sixty years before the date of that survey, which would indicate the year 1590. All the encroachments referred to in this complaint were upon the lord's wastes, including the Portmead and lords meadows (Waunarlwydd). Some of the encroachments were of remarkable extent, as for example, 200 acres near St. David's ditch, which was the western boundary of the borough. It is interesting to identify some of the places named in the complaint. For instance, Carn llwyd and Gwaun y llefrith are the commons of Trewyddfa; Gors fawr is the marsh on the bounds of Swansea and Loughor parishes, adjoining Waunarlwydd; Cors y Cob is the marsh near Pont y Cobb, or Cobb's bridge; Keven y fforest is just north of Penllergaer, although there are two holdings of this name; and Rid vugh is, without doubt, Nhyd-fuwch, and the encroachment was from Gorseinon common.

To this earl Edward, James I. granted, in 1607, 'in consideration of the good, faithful, and acceptable services to us heretofore manifoldly done and performed by our well-beloved and faithful cousin and counsellor Edward,' etc., that he and his heirs should have within (*inter alia*) 'his borough, castle, and manor of Swansey, Oystermouth, and Lloughore, and also within all that his lordship and land of Gower and Kilvey, and within his manor of Kithull, Triudva, Limon, Penard, and Westgower, by his bailiffs'—

The full return of all writs of assize, novel disseisin, mort d'ancestre and attainder, also of all other writs, mandates, precepts, bills, of us, our heirs, and successors, and of our justices and commissioners for the prosecuting of whatsoever suit; of summonses of the exchequer and other estreats, and of executions of the same; and that no sheriff or other officer or minister whatsoever shall intermeddle himself concerning such returns or executions, nor shall they enter the said castles, manors, lordships, lands, and boroughs, for doing execution unless it be in default of the earl's bailiff.

The earl was also to have all fines assessed for licences to accord of and from all lands and tenements in the lordship, etc., and all fines, issues, amerciaments, redemptions, pains and forfeitures, as well of his men as of the tenants and resiants within the lordship, etc., in all courts of the king (which are set forth in full); and the earl was to have and levy for his own benefit such amerciaments, fines, etc., as to the king should belong; also all goods and chattels of felons, fugitives, and outlaws, all treasure found and to be confiscated within the lordship, etc.; also that the men, tenants, etc., should not be brought into any plea in the county or other courts before the sheriffs, or be attached in their chattels taken by them.

The earl was also to have and constitute his own proper coroners in the lordship, borough, etc., with full power and authority of their offices, and no coroner of the king should intermeddle, etc.; the earl might have his clerks of the markets in the lordship and borough, who should have the same full powers 'which to the office of clerk of the market of our household belong;' he might have, hold, and execute before his steward all such pleas and other things 'which to the office and court of admiralty do in any manner belong,' together with the fines, amerciaments, etc.; arising, 'in manner as the admiral of the king could have.'

The earl was also to have wreck of the sea, wharfage, and tolls within the lordship, boroughs, etc., and also by his steward have and hold all courts baron and courts leet, view of frankpledge, and all fairs, markets, tolls, and other liberties and privileges, and that no officer of the king should sit within the lordship, etc., to inquire concerning any things arising therein.

Finally the earl was also to have 'all and all manner of wines and tuns of wines called "prise wynes" of whatsoever kind 'within the borough of Swanzey and the lordship and manor of Gower, and within any port or creek of the sea to the said borough or lordship appertaining; also the butlerage of all wines therein, and all profits and advantages of the butlerage, to hold the same of the king in free soccage, and rending therefor 2s. 6d. for every tun of prisage wines brought into the ports, creeks, etc., and 2s. for every tun of butlerage wines, to be paid to the chief butler of England.

There need be no doubt that the grant by the king of these valuable privileges and immunities to the earl in the borough of Swansea and the lordship of Gower arose out of a real regard for the earl and his ancestors. We have not the space at command to enumerate the many services rendered by the earls of Worcester to the crown, nor to indicate the intimacy with which they associated with the person of the king; suffice it to say that a long line of the heads of the family had been devotedly attached to successive monarchs, and that subsequent earls and marquises of Worcester and dukes of Beaufort have ever since been firm adherents and loyal servants of the crowned heads.

This earl Edward died on the 3rd March, 1627, and was succeeded by his son Henry, whose mother was Elizabeth, daughter of Francis, earl of Huntingdon.

To Henry, fifth earl of Worcester, we have not the space in which worthily to pay that tribute for his courage and loyalty displayed during the troublous times of the civil wars between the parliamentary and royalist forces which should ever be accorded to him. We can say no more than that he was a devoted adherent to Charles I., and held his castle of Raglan against the parliamentarians for four years at his own private charge. In acknowledgement of his many services, the king, in 1643, advanced the earl to the dignity of marquess of Worcester.

Amongst the muniments at Badminton is still preserved a letter addressed by the king to the marquess in August, 1644, acknowledging 'the great affection which you and your son have expressed unto me by eminent services,' and promising that, 'as soon as I shall confer the order of the garter upon any, you shall receive it as a testimonial of my being your assured constant friend Charles R.' And there is also there another letter, written in the same month, accompanying which is the following communication addressed 'to our attorney or solicitor-general for the time being:'—

'Charles R. Our will and pleasure is that you prepare a bill for our signature, for creating our right trusty and entirely-beloved cousin Henry, Marquis of Worcester, Duke of Somerset, to him and the heirs male of his body issuing, with all the privileges and immunities thereunto belonging, and with a grant of an annuity of fifty pounds yearly, to be paid to him and them, out of our Customs of Swansea, in our County of Glamorgan, for the support of the said dignity, for which this shall be your sufficient warrant. Given at our Court in Oxford, the sixth day of January, in the twentieth year of our reign.'

In the closing period of this gallant marquess's life, in 1645, a large portion of his estates had been confiscated by parliament, and later on settled on the lord general Oliver Cormwell.[9] This included (as enumerated in a later act of parliament dated 16th July 1651,[10] for the sale of other portions of the estate):

The manors and lordships of Anglicana Gower, Wallicana Gower, Swansey, Kilvey, Supraboscos, Oystermouth, Pennard, Lougher, Kythul *alias* Kitle, Trewithrah *alias* Triveday (Trewyddva), and Lunnon *alias* Ilston, with their and every of their rights, members, and appurtenances in the county of Glamorgan; and also the advowsons and rights of patronage of the churches of the several parishes of Gower and Swansey, with their and either of their rights, members, and appurtenances, 'which late were the property of Henry, late earl of Worcester, a popish recusant, and hath borne arms, etc., against, etc.'

The parliamentary report upon the estate of the marquess valued the seignory of Gower at £672 15s. 9d. per annum, but it is singular that, whilst making it a gift *inter alia* to the lord general, parliament should have overlooked settlements of 1627 and 1631, by which Gower was limited to what were then the usual uses in strict settlement, the effect of which was to make the seignory successively during their lives the estate of Earl Henry, and his son Edward, with remainder in tail to the latter's son, Henry, who on his grandfather's death, was known by the courtesy title of lord Herbert.

As to the delinquency of the marquess of Worcester and his son, the young lord Herbert was only about sixteen years of age at the time of the confiscation of the estates, and, so it was clearly demonstrated, from the time when he began to take part in public affairs, he espoused the cause in resistance to which his family had made such sacrifices, and actually sat in Cromwell's parliament and council of state, conforming also to the religion of those in power.[11]

Of Cromwell's association with the borough of Swansea and the lordship of Gower we shall write later on, but in 1648 he settled Gower and other estates upon Henry Cromwell, on his marriage. Cromwell died on the 3rd September, 1658, and the feeble tenure of the protectorate by his son Richard concluded on the 22nd May following, when he dissolved parliament. Probably Henry Cromwell continued to hold the lordship of Gower until the Restoration, on the 29th June, 1661, and the consequent reinstatement of the rightful owner.

Thus from 1645 until 1661 the lordship of Gower was alienated from the family of Worcester. In the meanwhile Edward, second marquess of Worcester, had succeeded to his father's title on his death in 1646. He too had been a sturdy supporter of the king, who, before his succession, addressed him as earl of Glamorgan, and granted him the almost unique distinction of entrusting him with blank patents under the great seal for creating titles from baronet to marquess, a privilege which he resigned in 1660. He died on the 3rd April, 1667, and his tomb in Raglan church styles him marquess and earl of Worcester, and baron Herbert of Raglan, Chepstow, and Gower.

To him succeeded Henry, third Marquis, K.G., who throughout the troublous times of the civil war, and until now, had been known as lord Herbert. He married Mary, daughter to lord Cahil, and widow of Henry, lord Beauchamp. He was elected Lord President of Wales and the

Marches, and was created duke of Beaufort in 1682. In this capacity of President he made an almost regal and singularly spectacular 'Progress' through Wales, a record of which by Thomas Dinely is preserved at Badminton, and has been published in *facsimile*.

His descendants, dukes of Beaufort and barons Herbert of Raglan, Chepstow, and Gower, have been:

1699. Henry, K.G., died 1714.

1714. Henry, K.G., died 1745.

1745. Charles Noel, died 1756.

1756. Henry, K.G., died 1803.

1803. Henry Charles, K.G., died 1835.

1835. Henry, K.G., died 1853.

1853. Henry Chas. Fitzroy, K.G., P.C., died 1899.

1899. Henry Adelbert Wellington Fitzroy, died 1925.

1925 Henry Hugh Arthur Fitzroy.

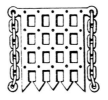

[1] *Baronage,* Vol. ii., p. 293

[2] 'Those times' were in some respects patterns of unrestrained misconduct in high life. The lawless manners of the period are demonstrated by an outrage committed upon the lady Margaret Malefaunt, widow of Sir Thomas, of Wenvoe and St. George, Glamorgan, which Thomas died the 8th May, 1438. Lewis Leyson, 'late of Glamorgan', undertook, as the trusted friend of her late husband, to convey the widow to her mother Jane Astley. But declaring that divers enemies lay in wait for her, she was made to travel for two days, from Upton Castle, Pembrokeshire, till they came 'by a park side called ye park of Prys (Park le Bruce) w'ynne the lordship of Gower,' when, as they came out of the Park, 'a great bushment' (ambush) of men in manner of war arrayed, with swords drawn made 'a great affray and assault' upon her, smiting her on the arm, and beating her servants. She was carried into 'the mountains' and kept without food 'till she was nigh dede'. After many days they came to Gilbert Turberville's place at Tythegstone, near Bridgend, where after Turberville and the local priest joined Leyson in appealing to her to marry him, Leyson 'hadd her yn to a chambr' withyn a strong Towr, and yer agaynst hur will ravished hur, and felonly lay by hur, she crying at all times after help and socour and none couth have.' The charge is set forth in a petition printed in *Arch. Camb.* 1852. p. 211.

[3] *Archaeological Journal,* x. 53, where Katherine is referred to in the will of the countess of Devon, 1527.

[4] The countess of Worcester (Elizabeth, d. of Sir Anthony Browne, knight) was one of four ladies who attended queen Anne Boleyn at her coronation dinner. To-day her office would appear menial, for she and the widowed countess of Oxford stood beside the queen's chair, and 'divers times in the dinner time did hold a fine cloth before the queen's face when she list to spit or do otherwise at her pleasure.' The two other gentlewomen sat at the queen's feet under the table! The earl of Worcester in his barge attended the queen's barge as she proceeded from Greenwich to the Tower. (Letters and Papers, For. and Dom. 1533, p. 278.) In 1533, the earl was one of four gentlemen who carried her gifts before the princess Elizabeth at her christening, three days after her birth; and in 1536 he was one of the peers who tried and convicted queen Anne Boleyn.

[5] The abbot and monastery of Neath had, it has already been shewn, many interests in Gower. The *valor ecclesiasticus* of 26th Henry VIII. (1534-5), of the abbey of Neath, printed in Dugdale's *Monasticon* (Vol. v., p. 260), includes:— 'In the Diocese of Saynt David in Gower—The Grange of Pauylond, 15s.; Too Werys within the Water of Tawey, 1s. Grange of Courte Carney, 15s.; Walterstone, 3li 2s.; Kellylybyan, 4li; Glynlygnewre (Glyn llwchwr), 6li. Spiritualities there, tithing of Courte Carney, 2li; Llandylo Talapont, 5li 6s. 8d.'

[7] The witnesses to the delivery of possession, named at the end of this document, are:— Richard Yoroeth, prepositus of the ville de Swanzey, Roger Jenkin, John Philip Harry, John Thomas Flemyng, Morgan John ap Hopkin, John ap Jevan Goch, Rhys ap Hopkyn David echan, Robert Phillipp of Swanzey, Rhys ap John ap Jevan, Roger Landegg, John William David ap Howel, and many others.

[8] The complaints contained in this document concerned encroachments upon the lord's wastes and moors, but the possession of property in Swansea by private owners is a subject which calls for an interesting and profitable investigation. The disappearance of the lord's demesne lands commenced at a very early period, as the record of the inquisition into the alienation of properties in Swansea and Gower by the De Breoses (see Vol. i., p. 322) clearly proves. The inquisition may have been brought about by a complaint of the earl of Warwick, who was a claimant for the lordship, that whilst he was pursuing his claim the lord occupant was distributing the lordship amongst his friends and servants. A list of the alienated lands

contained in the record points to a considerable distribution of land in Swansea prior to 1319, and the deed of foundation of the Hospital of St. David's reciting many gifts of local lands indicates how, in 1331, sites in the town had come into the possession of private persons, and were now donated to the endowment of the Hospital.

[9] 'A Survey of the Seignory or Lo'pp of Gower, with the several members thereof,' was begun the 27th August, 1650, by Bussy Mansell, and others, under a commission given them by 'the Right Hon'ble Oliver Cromwell, Lord G'nrall of the Parliam'ts forces.'

[10] The original grant is in the muniment-room at Badminton. It is dated 4th April, 24 Charles I., 1649, and conveys the lordship of Gower, the property of the marquis of Worcester, from the Long Parliament to Oliver Cromwell as lieutenant-general of Fairfax's army. The grant purports to be from Charles I., whose effigy fills the area of the initial letter 'C,' at the commencement of the deed; and at the foot, separately, is 'Per ordinationem parliamenti.'

[11] Marsh's *Annals of Chepstow Castle*, 1883, p. 230.

Appendix

Some publications since 1932, relevant to W. H. Jones' Volume II.

B. G. Charles & H. D. Emanuel, 'Welsh Records in the Hereford Capitular Archives', *National Library of Wales Journal* VII, Summer 1953.

W. R. B. Robinson, 'An analysis of a Minister's Account for the Borough of Swansea for 1449', *Bulletin of the Board of Celtic Studies* XXII,2, May 1967.

W. R. B. Robinson, 'The litigation of Edward, Earl of Worcester, concerning Gower, 1590 to 1596', *Bulletin of the Board of Celtic Studies* XXII,4, and XXIII,1, 1968.

J. Beverley Smith, T. B. Pugh & W. R. B. Robinson, 'The Lordship of Gower and Kilvey', and also Ralph A. Griffiths & W. R. B. Robinson, 'The Medieval Boroughs of Glamorgan and Medieval Swansea', both in *The Glamorgan County History* III, *The Middle Ages*, Cardiff 1971.

F. V. Emery, 'The Norman Conquest and the Medieval Period', W. G. Balchin (ed.) *Swansea and its Region*, Swansea 1971.

Ralph A. Griffiths, *The Principality of Wales in the later Middle Ages*, Cardiff 1972.

Edith Evans & C. J. Spurgeon, *Swansea Castle and the Medieval Town*, Swansea 1983.

W. S. K. Thomas, *The History of Swansea from Rover Settlement to the Restoration*, Llandysul, 1990.

Glanmor Williams, 'Before the Industrial Revolution', G. Williams (ed.) *Swansea, an Illustrated History*, Swansea 1990.

Various authors, in Ralph A. Griffiths (ed.) *The City of Swansea, Challenges & Change*, (British Association Swansea volume), Stroud 1990.

Royal Commission on Ancient and Historical Monuments in Wales, *Glamorgan Inventory* III, 1a, *The Early Castles*, London 1991.

Bernard Morris, *Swansea Castle*, Swansea 1992 (forthcoming).

INDEX
Prepared, 1992, by Gerald Gabb

General

Leather, 78
Lime kilns, 71
Llandaff, 16, 23
Locks, 30, 39

Magor, 2
Malt, 30
Margam, 1, 2, 80
Margam Abbey, 13, 61
Masons, 39, 42
Meadows (and see Redmead), 25, 29, 38,
  49, 57, 58, 71, 81, 82
Mountain meadow, 29

Neath (Neth, Neeth, Nyth, Nedeslonde), 1,
  2, 3, 4, 5, 6, 7, 59, 75, 79
Neath Abbey, 12-13, 77, 88
Neath, John of, 28, 30, 35
Neath, Leyshon, abbot of, 77
Neath, Reding (Rhyddings ?) in, 8

Parchment, 41
Paper, 41
Pasture, 80
Pembrokeshire, 2
Portreeve (prepositus, preposito, mayor),
  12,   31, 34, 55, 70, 72, 88
Portreeves:
  John Bount, 29, 55
  John Cradock, 70, 72, 73
  David Fourboure, 72
  William Mathew, 31, 41, 57-58
  John Thomas, 72
  Richard Yoroeth, 88

Salmon, 30
Scotland, 10, 11, 22
Smiths, 78

Tanning, 78
Tiling, 39, 42

Wentllwch, 2
Wine, 46, 84
Wrecks, 84

Ystrad Towy (Istrad Towy, Strathawy), 17

People

Adam le Coron'r, 4
Astley, Jane, 88
Aston, Robert de, 22
Athelard, William, 28
Avene, Sir John de, 19
  Thomas de, 15, 18-19, 19-20

Baker, Felicia, 29
  Felix, 70-71
  John, 28
Baptist, John, 56
Barett, Harry, 77
Bars (or Bate ?), William, 28, 30
Basset, family, 22
  James, 22
  John, 22
Beauchamp (Bello campo),
  family, 13
  Guy, 25
  John, 25
  Katherine, 14, 24, 25
  Rainburn, 24, 33
  Richard, Earl of Warwick, 54, 60
  Roger, 24
  Thomas, Earl of Warwick (d. 1369),
    13-14, 15, 20, 23, 24-5, 33
  Thomas, Earl of Warwick (d. 1401),
    25-27, 33
Beaufort, Dukes of, 10, 87 (and see
  Somerset)
Beaumond, Sir John, 26
Beaumont, Roger de, Earl of Warwick, 15
  Waleran de, Earl of Warwick,
    21, 23
  William de, Earl of Warwick,
    15, 18, 21, 23
Benet, Richard, 57
Bere, de la (de la Biere, Delabere),
  family, 7-8, 51
  Adam, 7
  David, 3, 7
  Isobel, 7
  Sir John, 7, 13, 29, 30, 31, 33, 41, 47,
    51
  Peter, 3, 4, 8
  Richard, 13
  Roger, 7
Berkeley, Sir William, 49

Bernard, William, 56
Blake, John, 28
Blew, Thomas, 4
Bloyon (Gloyon ?), Ralph, 10, 22
Bohun, Edward de, 7
Bokyngham, John de, bishop of Lincoln, 25
Boner, John, 28, 40
Bortheward, Thomas, 31
Bosenho (Bosentro), Roger de, 5
Boston, Thomas, 53
Boterwyk, Richard, 4
Bougan, Walter, 5
Bount (Bunt), John, 29, 55
Box, Walter le, 4, 5
Braas, Robert, 40
Breos, Alina de, 3, 9, 10, 11, 18, 19, 22
   John de, 14, 16, 19
   William de (d. 1211), 16-17, 19, 21,
   67
   William de (d. 1290), 13, 16, 17
   William de (d. 1326), 1, 8, 9, 10, 12,
   16, 17, 18, 32, 34, 53
Bruno the Jew, 21
Burdegala, Oliver de, 7
Burgh, Elizabeth de, 18
   Hubert de, 16, 19
Burghersh, Bartholemew, 11
Butler, John, 7

Cadogan, William ap, 4
Canon, Thomas, 28
Carman, Robert, 5
Cauntyngton, Griffith ap, 4
Chambers (Chambour), Thomas, 70, 72
Charles, Thomas, 28-29, 31, 35, 66, 70
Chaundeler, Roger le, 4
Chaundos, Roger, 9
Clerke, Nicholas, 70
Clif, Henry de, 3
Cnoyl (and see Knoille),
   Peter le, 22
   Richard le, 22
   Robert le, 22
   William le, 22
Colet, Richard, 26
Conneway, Henry, 29, 71
Constable, John, 29
Coppa, David, 40
Cornys, Thomas 28
Coron'r, Adam le, 4

Corow, Robert, 29
Courtenay, Peter, 46
Cradoc(k), family, 7-8, 22, 34-35, 57
   David, 7-8
   Elizabeth, 7-8
   Jevan ap, 28, 34
   John, 70, 72, 73
   Sir Mathew, 22, 35, 36, 58-59,
   73, 76, 79
   Matilda (Maud), 59
   Rees, 59
   Richard, 36
   Thomas ap Jevan ap, 41

David, John, 4, 8, 39
   John ap, 77
   Rhys ap Hopkyn, 88
Davy, John, 70
   Richard, 30
Dawkin (Dawkyn),
   family, 82
   Elizabeth, 80, 81, 82
   Hopkyn, 77, 82
   Jenkin, 82
   Thomas, 70
   William (i), 81, 82
   William (ii), 82
   William ap Thomas, 70
Delamare — see Mare, de la
Despenser, family, 22
   Eleanor le, 7
   Hugh le, the elder, 1, 3
   Hugh le, the younger, 1, 3, 7,
   18
Dier (Dieghere), Sir John, 28, 29, 30, 35
Ditton, Henrici de, 4
Donne (Don, Doon, Dwnn),
   family, 69
   Bernard, 4
   Geoffrey, 57
   Henry, 46, 51
   Jenkyn David, 80
   John, 4
   Sir John, 69, 73
   Rees ap Jenkin ap Jevan, 82
   Robert, 4

Doubeney (Doudeney), Agnes, 28
Dunnyng, Robert, 22
Duphous, John, 4

95

Meyrick (Meuric, Meuryk), Jevan ap, 2
   Morgan ap, 4
   Patric ap, 5
   Robert ap Williams ap, 29
   Thomas ap, 77
Montacute, William de, 1, 11, 60
More, Richard, 40
Morgan, Jevan ap, 2
   John David, 77
   Morgan John, 80, 82
   Rice, ap, 69-70
Moris (Mees ?), John, 29
Mortimer, Edmund, 42
Mowbray, Alina de (Née de Breos, later de
   Peshale), 3, 9, 10, 11, 18, 19, 22
   Anne de, Duchess of Norfolk,
     64, 65, 68
   Catherine de, 55
   Elizabeth de, Duchess of
     Norfolk, 28, 30, 37, 38, 41, 53,
     54, 60, 66-67
   John de (d. 1322), 3, 8, 9, 22
   John de (d. 1361), 10, 11, 12, 13,
     15, 18, 19, 33
   John de, 2nd Duke of Norfolk
     (d. 1432), 47, 53, 54, 55, 57, 73
   John de, 3rd Duke of Norfolk
     (d. 1461), 57, 58, 59, 61, 62,
     63, 68
   John de, 4th Duke of Norfolk
     (d. 1476), 69, 70
   Thomas de, Earl of Nottingham,
     1st Duke of Norfolk (d. 1399),
     26, 27, 28, 30, 32, 34, 53, 54,
     71
   Thomas de, Earl Marshall
     (d. 1405), 47, 53, 54

Neath, John de, 28, 30, 35
Newburgh, de — see Beaumont, de
Nicholl, Richard Fitz, 53
Norfolk, Dukes, Duchesses, Earls of — see
   Mowbrey, de
Norys, Thomas, 56

Osbarne (Caebern ?), Thomas, 29, 30
Owen (Owein), John ap, 81
   Roger ap, 77
   Thomas ap, 77

Pacy, John, 55
Parkyn, John, 77
Paty, John, 41, 48
Pederton, Walter de, 16, 17, 18
Penbrugge (Penrigg), Robert de, 2, 4
Penres (Penress, Penrys, Penrees),
   family, 13, 22, 50
   Isabella de (née Stakepole), 22, 28,
     35
   Johanna de, 13
   Sir John de (i), 5, 13, 22
   Sir John de (ii), 31, 35, 50
   Richard de, 4, 10, 22, 33, 35
   Robert de (i), 2, 4, 8, 13, 35, 50
   Sir Robert de, 50
Penry, Owen, 80
Percy, Thomas, Earl of Worcester, 42
Perkin, Robert, 29
Perot, Richard, 40
Peshale, Sir Richard de, 3, 9, 10, 19, 22
Petous, David, 5
Phillip the hermit, 56
Phillip (Phelipp), John, 4
   Meyryck, ap, 26
   Resi ap, 57
   Robert, 88
Philpott ? (Ph'ot), Dankyn, 28, 35
Pistor, John, 31
Poket, John, 29
Poret, Henry, 28
Porter, William le, 4
Powcock, John, 70
Price, John, 81-82

Quart, John, 5

Reding, Simon de, 4
Rees Du (Res Dwy), 4, 8
Rees (Res, Ries, Resi),
   Hopkin ap, 69, 73
   Jevan ap Gwyllym ap, 41
   Maelgon Filio (Crik), 14
   Phillip, 4
   Phillip John ap, 80, 82
   Thomas, 82
   Thomas ap, 28
Richards (Richard, Ricard), Hoell ap, 40
   John William David ap, 80, 82
   William Thomas ap, 80-81

The Town of Swansea

The Lordship of Gower

101

Postscript

This Royal Institution of South Wales publication has been prepared and edited by Bernard Morris and the index has been compiled by Gerald Gabb. Thanks are due to Miss Joan Wilton (for help with the glossary on page 6), to Dr. David Painting (for initial information on W. H. Jones' life) and to Mr. D. S. Taylor (for providing the source of the photograph of the author on page xii). All are members of the Royal Institution.

We appreciate the work of our printers, Gwasg Morgannwg, of Neath Abbey, and of Mr. Gareth Richards, Proprietor, who have taken in their stride a complex and sometimes unusual text.

The Royal Institution of South Wales was founded in 1835 and is an independent learned voluntary society. Through many of its activities it aims to support and promote the Swansea Museum, which is run and funded by the Swansea City Council.

It is hoped that this publication of the second volume of W. H. Jones' *History* will be just the first of a series of reference and general interest works relating to Swansea and West Glamorgan to be produced by the Royal Institution. These would have the aim of making more readily available unpublished local records and the results of work on all aspects of the Museum's collections and interests.

In addition to its other activities, the Royal Institution arranges a varied programme of evening lectures and some social events. New members are welcome and enquiries should be addressed to the Membership Secretary, R.I.S.W., c/o Swansea Museum, Victoria Road, Swansea SA1 1SN.